H E I N E M A N N

S H A K E S P E A R E

Romeo and Juliet

edited by John Seely

with drama notes and activities by
Rick Lee

Series Editor: John Seely

*In association with the RSA
Shakespeare in Schools Project*

The RSA Shakespeare in Schools Project

The **Heinemann Shakespeare Series** has been developed in association with the **RSA Shakespeare in Schools Project**. Schools in the project have trialled teaching approaches to make Shakespeare accessible to students of all ages and ability levels.

John Seely has worked with schools in the project to develop the unique way of teaching Shakespeare to 11- to 16-year-olds found in **Heinemann Shakespeares.**

The project is a partnership between RSA (Royal Society for the encouragement of Arts, Manufactures & Commerce) Leicestershire County Council and the Groby family of schools in Leicestershire. It is co-ordinated by the Knighton Fields Advisory Centre for Drama and Dance.

We would particularly like to acknowledge Brookvale High School for the contribution to *Romeo and Juliet.*

Heinemann Educational Publishers
Halley Court, Jordan Hill, Oxford OX2 8EJ
a division of Reed Educational & Professional Publishing Ltd
OXFORD MELBOURNE AUCKLAND
JOHANNESBURG BLANTYRE GABORONE
IBADAN PORTSMOUTH (NH) USA CHICAGO

Introduction, notes and activities © John Seely and Rick Lee 1993

Published in the *Heinemann Shakespeare* series 1993

03 02 01 00 99
16 15 14 13

A catalogue record for this book is available from the British Library on request.
ISBN 0 435 19201 9

Cover design by Miller Craig and Cocking
Cover photograph from Donald Cooper

Typeset by Taurus Graphics, Kidlington, Oxon

Printed by Clays Ltd, St Ives plc

Contents

Explorations

Introduction: Using this book

This is more than just an edition of Romeo and Juliet with a few notes. It is a complete guide to studying and enjoying the play.

It begins with an introduction to Shakespeare's theatre, and to the story and characters of the play.

At the end of the book there is guidance on studying the play:
- how to keep tracks of things as you work
- how to take part in a range of drama activities
- understanding Shakespeare's language
- exploring the main themes of conflict, love and destiny
- studying the characters
- how to write about the play.

There are also practice questions for Key Stage 3 and Key Stage 4 and a glossary of specialist words you need when working on the play.

The central part of the book is, of course, the play itself. Here there are several different kinds of help on offer:

Summary: at the top of each page there is a short summary of what happens on that page.

Grading: alongside the text is a shaded band to help you when working on the play:

1 This is very important text that you probably need to spend extra time on.
2 This is text that you need to read carefully.
3 This is text that you need to spend less time on.

Notes: difficult words, phrases and sentences are explained in simple English

Extra summaries: for the 'white' text the notes are replaced by numbered summaries that give more detail than the ordinary page-by-page summaries.

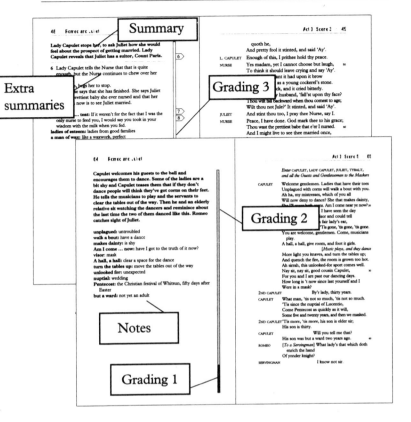

Activities

Every few scenes there is a section containing things to do, helping you focus on the scenes you have just read:

- questions to make sure you have understood the story
- discussion points about the themes and characters of the play
- drama activities
- character work
- close study to help you focus on a section of the text in more detail
- writing activities

Shakespeare's theatre

Heavens (A)
the roof above the stage,
supported by pillars. Characters
could be lowered to the stage
during the play

Gallery (B)
used for action on an upper level
(or, if not, for the musicians)

Inner space (C)
curtained area that could be
opened up to show a new scene

*Standing space for
audience*

Doors (D)
used by the actors, leading from
the stage to the tiring house
(dressing rooms)

Stage (E)
the acting area was very
big and had trapdoors
so that actors could enter
from underneath the
stage floor.

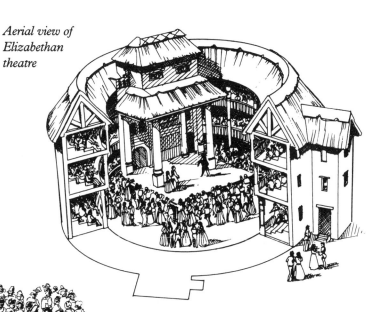

Aerial view of Elizabethan theatre

A scene from Romeo and Juliet, showing both the inner stage and the gallery in use for the action of the play.

When you have studied the play you should be able to work out exactly which moment in the play this shows.

Going to the theatre in Shakespeare's day

Theatre-going was very popular in Elizabethan London, but it was very different from going to a play today. It was like a cross between going to a football match and going to the theatre. The playhouses were open air and as there was no artificial lighting plays were performed in daylight, normally in the afternoon.

Places were not reserved, so people had to arrive in plenty of time - often more than an hour before the play was due to start. They paid a penny to get into the playhouse, so it was not cheap, since a penny was about one twelfth of a day's wages for a skilled workman. Your penny let you into the large open yard surrounding the stage. The audience here had to stand, looking up at the actors (the stage was 1.5-1.8 metres above the ground). If people wanted a seat, then they had to pay another penny or twopence. This gave admission to the tiers of seating surrounding the yard, and also meant that you had a roof over your head, in case it started to rain. People with even more money could pay to have a seat in an enclosed room. So people of all incomes and social classes attended the theatre and paid for the kind of seating they wanted.

While the audience was waiting for the play to begin they had time to meet friends, talk, eat and drink - in fact people used to continue to enjoy themselves in this way while the play was being performed. But Elizabethan audiences were knowledgeable and enthusiastic. Watching a play was an exciting experience; although the stage was very big, the theatre was quite small, so no one was far from the actors. When an actor had a soliloquy (solo speech) he could come right into the middle of the audience and speak his thoughts in a natural, personal way. At the other extreme whole battles could be enacted, complete with cannon fire,

thunder and lightning and loud military music on the large
stage with its three different levels.

There was no painted stage scenery, so the audience had to
use their imagination to picture the location of each scene.
To help them, Shakespeare made sure that the characters'
speeches contained vivid indications of when and where a
scene took place. The lack of scenery to be moved about
also meant that scene could follow scene without any break.
On the other hand, the theatre companies spared no
expense on costumes and furniture and other properties;
plays also had live music performed by players placed
either in the auditorium close to the stage, or in the gallery
above it.

Altogether Londoners especially must have considered that
going to the theatre was an exciting and important part of
their lives; it is believed that up to a fifth of them went to the
theatre regularly. Shakespeare and the company in which he
became a shareholder, the Lord Chamberlain's Men,
worked hard and became wealthy men.

The story of the play

Romeo and Juliet are the children of two wealthy families in Verona, the Montagues and the Capulets. The two families have been feuding for years. At the beginning of the play, Paris has said that he wants to marry Juliet, and Romeo is unhappily in love with Rosaline. At a feast given by Juliet's father, Romeo and Juliet meet and fall in love, not knowing that they are members of rival families. After the feast, Romeo goes back to the Capulets' house and sees Juliet on her balcony. They declare their love, agree to marry, and arrange to meet the following day at Friar Lawrence's cell. The next day they are married by Friar Lawrence and make arrangements for Romeo to come to Juliet that night.

Unknown to Romeo, Tybalt, a Capulet, has seen Romeo at the feast and vowed to take revenge at this insult to his family pride. Later that day he meets Mercutio, a friend of Romeo and relative of the Prince of Verona, with Benvolio, a Montague. Tybalt demands to know where Romeo is and Mercutio taunts him into a fight. Romeo arrives on the scene and tries to stop the fight. In the process, Mercutio is killed and Tybalt escapes. Realising what he has done, Romeo vows to get revenge for his friend's death. When Tybalt returns he kills him and then is persuaded by Benvolio to flee. The Prince sentences Romeo to banishment.

Both Juliet and Romeo are dismayed at the sentence. Romeo is calmed by Friar Lawrence, who tells him to go to Mantua, where the Friar will keep him informed of what happens. The Friar assures Juliet that things will work out eventually. The two lovers meet that night to say goodbye. Immediately after Romeo has gone, Juliet's parents tell her that they have decided she should marry Paris in two days' time. Horrified, she refuses and her father says that if she will not marry Paris he will disown her.

The next day Juliet goes to Friar Lawrence for advice. He gives her a drug which, he says, will make her sleep and look as if she is dead. When she awakes he will rescue her from the family vault and take her to Romeo in Mantua. Meanwhile he will send a message to Romeo. As the Capulets prepare for the wedding, Juliet takes the drug. Amidst great family grief, she is buried.

Friar Lawrence's message fails to get to Romeo because of an outbreak of plague. Romeo hears news of the death of Juliet and resolves to poison himself. He returns to Verona and goes to Juliet's tomb. Paris is there; they fight and Paris is killed. After saying farewell to the 'dead' Juliet, Romeo takes the poison and dies. Juliet awakes and sees the dead body of her lover. She cannot live without Romeo and so stabs herself.

The Prince, Capulet, Lady Capulet and Montague arrive at the tomb. Friar Lawrence is brought to them and explains what has happened. In great grief, the two families realise that it is their feud that has led to their children's death. They are brought together in peace and agree to erect statues of the two lovers as a memorial and as a sign of their new harmony.

The characters of the play

THE 'NEUTRALS' (The Prince and his relatives)

Escalus, Prince of Verona

Mercutio

Paris, a wealthy young count

THE MONTAGUES

Montague

Lady Montague

Benvolio

ROMEO

Abraham, a servant

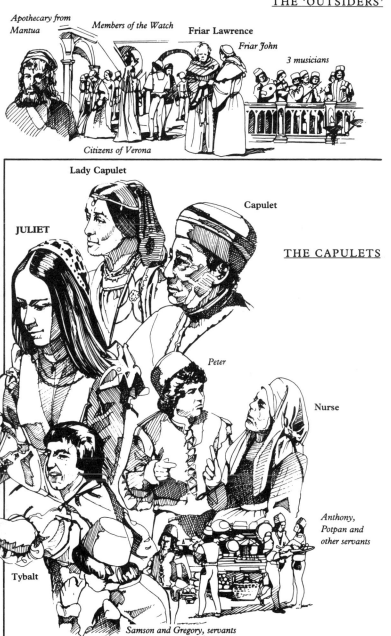

Apothecary from Mantua

Members of the Watch

Friar Lawrence

Friar John

3 musicians

Citizens of Verona

Lady Capulet

Capulet

JULIET

THE CAPULETS

Peter

Nurse

Anthony, Potpan and other servants

Tybalt

Samson and Gregory, servants

Romeo and Juliet

Characters

ESCALUS, Prince of Verona

PARIS, a nobleman, kinsman to the Prince

MONTAGUE
CAPULET } heads of two opposed Houses

SECOND CAPULET, cousin to Capulet

ROMEO, son to Montague

BENVOLIO, nephew to Montague and friend to Romeo

MERCUTIO, kinsman to the Prince and friend to Romeo

TYBALT, nephew to Lady Capulet

PETRUCHIO, a Capulet and friend to Tybalt

FRIAR LAWRENCE
FRIAR JOHN } Franciscans

BALTHASAR, servant to Romeo

ABRAHAM, servant to Montague

SAMPSON
GREGORY } servants to Capulet

PETER, a clown, servant to the Nurse

ANTHONY
POTPAN } servants to Capulet

AN APOTHECARY

PAGE to Paris

CHORUS

LADY MONTAGUE, wife to Montague

LADY CAPULET, wife to Capulet

JULIET, daughter to Capulet

NURSE to Juliet

Attendants, Citizens, Musicians, Servants, Watchmen.

SCENE *Verona; Mantua; Friar Lawrence's cell*

The prologue, spoken by one of the actors, introduces
the play and sums up what is going to happen: we
know from the very beginning that the play will end
in tragedy.

both alike in dignity: of similar (high) social standing
ancient grudge: an old disagreement
new mutiny: a new conflict
civil: they are civilians, not soldiers
From forth ... life: to these two ill-fated hostile families
   are born two lovers who are destined by the stars to
   disaster.
overthrows: deaths
but: except for
nought: nothing
two hours' ... stage: the subject matter of the play, lasting
   two hours. (In fact the play is considerably longer than
   two hours, but the expression is probably just meant to
   show that the play is not going to be boring.)

Prologue

CHORUS

Two households both alike in dignity,
In fair Verona where we lay our scene,
From ancient grudge break to new mutiny.
Where civil blood makes civil hands unclean.
From forth the fatal loins of these two foes
A pair of star-crossed lovers take their life;
Whose misadventured piteous overthrows
Doth with their death bury their parents' strife.
The fearful passage of their death-marked love,
And the continuance of their parents' rage,   10
Which, but their children's end, nought could remove,
Is now the two hours' traffic of our stage;
The which if you with patient ears attend,
What here shall miss, our toil shall strive to mend.

[*Exit*

In the heat of a summer's day in Verona, two servants from the house of Capulet swagger around the streets looking for trouble.

1 The two Capulet servants, Sampson and Gregory are in the mood for a fight. They are ready for trouble, especially from the Montagues.
2 Gregory teases Sampson that he's more likely to run away than to fight.
3 Sampson replies that he'll take on any Montague, male or female
4 Gregory points out that the feud is between the men.
5 Sampson says he doesn't care. He'll fight the men first and then 'deal with' the women.

1 >

2 >

3 >

4 >
5 >

Act one

Verona. A public place
Enter SAMPSON *and* GREGORY, *of the house of*
Capulet, with swords and bucklers

SAMPSON   Gregory, on my word we'll not carry coals.

GREGORY   No, for then we should be colliers.

SAMPSON   I mean, an we be in choler, we'll draw.

GREGORY   Ay, while you live, draw your neck out of collar.

SAMPSON   I strike quickly being moved.

GREGORY   But thou art not quickly moved to strike.

SAMPSON   A dog of the house of Montague moves me.

GREGORY   To move is to stir, and to be valiant is to stand.
           Therefore if thou art moved, thou runn'st
           away.   10

SAMPSON   A dog of that house shall move me to stand. I will
           take the wall of any man or maid of Montague's.

GREGORY   That shows thee a weak slave, for the weakest
           goes to the wall.

SAMPSON   'Tis true, and therefore women being the weaker
           vessels are ever thrust to the wall. Therefore I
           will push Montague's men from the wall, and
           thrust his maids to the wall.

GREGORY   The quarrel is between our masters and us their
           men.   20

SAMPSON   'Tis all one. I will show myself a tyrant. When I
           have fought with the men, I will be cruel with the
           maids–I will cut off their heads.

GREGORY   The heads of the maids?

SAMPSON   Ay, the heads of the maids, or their
           maidenheads–take it in what sense thou wilt.

They meet two servants from the house of Montague and begin to taunt them.

Quarrel: make a quarrel, start an argument.

marry: originally this was 'By the Virgin Mary', but it was only a mild expression (like 'indeed')

Let us ... our sides: let us stay on the right side of the law

list: wish

bite my thumb: a rude gesture. You put your thumb in your mouth and then withdrew it, clicking the nail against your upper front teeth.

Fear me not: I won't let you down

GREGORY	They must take it in sense that feel it.
SAMPSON	Me they shall feel while I am able to stand, and 'tis known I am a pretty piece of flesh.
GREGORY	'Tis well thou art not fish; if thou hadst, thou 30 hadst been poor-john. Draw thy tool, here comes of the house of Montagues.

Enter two other serving-men, ABRAHAM *and* BALTHASAR

SAMPSON	My naked weapon is out. Quarrel, I will back thee.
GREGORY	How, turn thy back and run?
SAMPSON	Fear me not.
GREGORY	No marry, I fear thee!
SAMPSON	Let us take the law of our sides, let them begin.
GREGORY	I will frown as I pass by, and let them take it as they list.
SAMPSON	Nay, as they dare. I will bite my thumb at them, 40 which is disgrace to them if they bear it.
ABRAHAM	Do you bite your thumb at us sir?
SAMPSON	I do bite my thumb sir.
ABRAHAM	Do you bite your thumb at us sir?
SAMPSON	[*Aside to Gregory*] Is the law of our side if I say 'Ay'.
GREGORY	[*Aside to Sampson*] No.
SAMPSON	No sir, I do not bite my thumb at you sir, but I bite my thumb sir.
GREGORY	Do you quarrel sir? 50
ABRAHAM	Quarrel sir? No sir.
SAMPSON	But if you do sir, I am for you. I serve as good a man as you.
ABRAHAM	No better.
SAMPSON	Well sir.

Enter BENVOLIO

The argument between the servants develops into a
fight. Benvolio, a Montague, tries to stop the fighting,
but Tybalt, one of the Capulets, arrives and attacks
him. Citizens come and try to stop the fighting but
then the leader of the Capulet family arrives and
wants to join in too. He is restrained by his wife.

kinsmen: relatives
washing blow: slashing out
Put up: sheathe
heartless hinds: a play on words. 'Heartless' means
without a male deer (hart) to protect them. 'Hinds' are
literally female deer, but also female servants.
I do but: I'm only
manage it to part: use it to separate
Clubs, bills ... partisans: Weapons. Bills and partisans
are kinds of pike (a long spear that was held and thrust,
rather than thrown).
A crutch: she means that rather than having a sword, he is
so old he ought to be asking for a crutch to support him.
in spite of: in hatred of
stir: move

GREGORY   [*Aside to Sampson*] Say 'better'; here comes one
of my master's kinsmen.

SAMPSON   Yes, better sir.

ABRAHAM   You lie.

SAMPSON   Draw if you be men. Gregory, remember thy   60
washing blow.   [*They fight*

BENVOLIO   Part fools.
Put up your swords, you know not what you do.

Enter TYBALT

TYBALT   What, art thou drawn among these heartless
        hinds?
Turn thee Benvolio, look upon thy death.

BENVOLIO   I do but keep the peace. Put up thy sword,
Or manage it to part these men with me.

TYBALT   What, drawn and talk of peace? I hate the word,
As I hate hell, all Montagues, and thee.
Have at thee coward!   [*they fight* 70

Enter OFFICER *and Citizens with clubs and partisans*

OFFICER   Clubs, bills, and partisans! Strike, beat them down.
Down with the Capulets! Down with the
Montagues!

Enter OLD CAPULET *in his gown, and* LADY CAPULET

CAPULET   What noise is this? Give me my long sword, ho!

L. CAPULET   A crutch, a crutch! Why call you for a sword?

CAPULET   My sword I say! Old Montague is come,
And flourishes his blade in spite of me.

Enter OLD MONTAGUE *and* LADY MONTAGUE

MONTAGUE   Thou villain Capulet! Hold me not, let me go.

L. MONTAGUE   Thou shalt not stir one foot to seek a foe.

Enter PRINCE ESCALUS, *with his train*

Just as the head of the house of Montague is also attempting to join the fray, the Prince of Verona arrives and quells the riot. He orders them all to put down their weapons and tells Capulet and Montague that if anyone ever disturbs the peace again in this way they will be executed. Benvolio tells Montague how the fight began.

Profaners ... steel: they have stained the steel of their swords with the blood of their fellow-citizens ('neighbours') and, in this way they have abused or polluted ('profaned') it.

pernicious: destructive

mistempered: a play on words. 'Temper' means (i) the toughness of a piece of metal after it has been tempered (ii) angry mood. So if the weapons are 'mistempered' they have been (i) made for the wrong purpose (ii) used in anger.

moved: angry

civil brawls: fights between citizens

bred of an airy word: started because of an unimportant remark

Cast by ... ornaments: put down the sober (and suitable) things they were carrying

Cankered: grown rusty (because they had not been used, since the citizens have been at peace and are not used to fighting)

cankered: mis-shapen (as in a cancer)

Your lives ... forfeit: you will be executed

our further pleasure: what else I have decided

1 Montague asks Benvolio how the fighting began.
2 Benvolio explains that it had already been started by servants of the two families before he arrived. He had tried to stop them, but Tybalt had attacked him; then the two of them fought until the Prince arrived.

PRINCE	Rebellious subjects, enemies to peace, 80
	Profaners of this neighbour-stained steel—
	Will they not hear?—What ho! You men, you beasts,
	That quench the fire of your pernicious rage
	With purple fountains issuing from your veins,
	On pain of torture, from those bloody hands
	Throw your mistempered weapons to the ground,
	And hear the sentence of your moved Prince.
	Three civil brawls bred of an airy word,
	By thee old Capulet, and Montague,
	Have thrice disturbed the quiet of our streets, 90
	And made Verona's ancient citizens
	Cast by their grave beseeming ornaments,
	To wield old partisans, in hands as old,
	Cankered with peace, to part your cankered hate.
	If ever you disturb our streets again,
	Your lives shall pay the forfeit of the peace.
	For this time all the rest depart away.
	You Capulet shall go along with me.
	And Montague, come you this afternoon,
	To know our further pleasure in this case, 100
	To old Freetown, our common judgment-place.
	Once more, on pain of death, all men depart.
	[*Exeunt all but Montague, Lady Montague, and Benvolio*
MONTAGUE	Who set this ancient quarrel new abroach?
	Speak nephew, were you by when it began?
BENVOLIO	Here were the servants of your adversary,
	And yours, close fighting ere I did approach.
	I drew to part them; in the instant came
	The fiery Tybalt, with his sword prepared,
	Which as he breathed defiance to my ears,
	He swung about his head and cut the winds, 110
	Who nothing hurt withal hissed him in scorn.
	While we were interchanging thrusts and blows,
	Came more and more and fought on part and part,
	Till the Prince came, who parted either part.

Lady Montague asks where her son, Romeo, is. Benvolio has seen him but Romeo wants to be left alone. No one seems to know what is the matter with him.

3   Lady Montague asks Benvolio if he has seen Romeo, her son.

4   Benvolio tells her that he did see Romeo very early that morning. He was walking alone in the woods just outside the city, but when he saw Benvolio he hid. So Benvolio left him alone.

5   Montague says he often goes out early like that, and seems very unhappy. As soon as the sun rises properly he comes home and shuts himself up in his room. He is concerned about his son's health.

6   Benvolio asks if he knows why Romeo is behaving like this.

7   Montague says that Romeo is so secretive it is impossible to find out what is wrong, but he would dearly like to know.

L. MONTAGUE O where is Romeo? Saw you him today?
Right glad I am he was not at this fray.

BENVOLIO Madam, an hour before the worshipped sun
Peered forth the golden window of the east,
A troubled mind drive me to walk abroad,
Where underneath the grove of sycamore, 120
That westward rooteth from this city side,
So early walking did I see your son.
Towards him I made; but he was ware of me,
And stole into the covert of the wood.
I, measuring his affections by my own,
Which then most sought where most might not
be found,
Being one too many by my weary self,
Pursued my humour, not pursuing his,
And gladly shunned who gladly fled from me.

MONTAGUE Many a morning hath he there been seen, 130
With tears augmenting the fresh morning's dew,
Adding to clouds more clouds with his deep sighs,
But all so soon as the all-cheering sun
Should in the farthest east begin to draw
The shady curtains from Aurora's bed,
Away from light steals home my heavy son,
And private in his chamber pens himself,
Shuts up his windows, locks fair daylight out,
And makes himself an artificial night.
Black and portentous must this humour prove, 140
Unless good counsel may the cause remove.

BENVOLIO My noble uncle, do you know the cause?

MONTAGUE I neither know it, nor can learn of him.

BENVOLIO Have you importuned him by any means?

MONTAGUE Both by myself and many other friends.
But he, his own affections' counsellor,
Is to himself–I will not say how true–
But to himself so secret and so close,
So far from sounding and discovery,

Romeo arrives and his parents withdraw. Benvolio asks him why he is so sad. Romeo explains that he is in love and feels completely confused.

8 Romeo appears. Benvolio suggests that his parents leave and promises that he will find out what is wrong. They agree to depart.

8 >

But new: only just

Not having ... short: The fact that I haven't got what would make time pass quickly if I did have it.

so gentle ... in proof: so gentle to look at turns out to be oppressive and cruel when we experience it.

whose view is muffled: Cupid the god of love was often painted as blindfolded

to his will: to getting his own way

Where shall we dine?: Romeo is, perhaps, trying to change the subject.

o brawling love ... sick health: at the time when Shakespeare wrote *Romeo and Juliet*, it was fashionable for poets to write of love using apparently impossible opposites like 'loving hate'. These opposites are called *oxymorons* (see Glossary). This part of the speech shows how confused Romeo's feelings are (or is it that he wants to *seem* confused?)

O anything of nothing first create!: Like the first thing to be made, created by God out of nothing

As is the bud bit with an envious worm,   150
Ere he can spread his sweet leaves to the air,
Or dedicate his beauty to the sun.
Could we but learn from whence his sorrows grow,
We would as willingly give cure as know.

Enter ROMEO

BENVOLIO	See where he comes. So please you step aside.
	I'll know his grievance or be much denied.
MONTAGUE	I would thou wert so happy by thy stay,
	To hear true shrift. Come madam, let's away.

         [Exeunt Montague and Lady Montague

BENVOLIO	Good morrow cousin.
ROMEO	Is the day so young?
BENVOLIO	But new struck nine.
ROMEO	Ay me, sad hours seem long. 160
	Was that my father that went hence so fast?
BENVOLIO	It was. What sadness lengthens Romeo's hours?
ROMEO	Not having that which having makes them short.
BENVOLIO	In love?
ROMEO	Out–
BENVOLIO	Of love?
ROMEO	Out of her favour where I am in love.
BENVOLIO	Alas that love, so gentle in his view,
	Should be so tyrannous and rough in proof!
ROMEO	Alas that love, whose view is muffled still, 170
	Should without eyes see pathways to his will.
	Where shall we dine? O me, what fray was here?
	Yet tell me not, for I have heard it all.
	Here's much to do with hate, but more with love.
	Why then, o brawling love, o loving hate,
	O any thing of nothing first create!
	O heavy lightness, serious vanity,
	Mis-shapen chaos of well-seeming forms,
	Feather of lead, bright smoke, cold fire, sick health,

Benvolio tries without success to discover the name of the girl Romeo has fallen in love with. Romeo explains that she is not in love with him.

This love ... in this: this is how he is experiencing love, but he is not enjoying it.

coz: cousin (also used to mean 'uncle, nephew, niece, brother-in-law).

1 Romeo asks Benvolio why he is sad.
2 Benvolio explains that is because of Romeo's depression.
3 Romeo replies that that is what love is like: if Benvolio allows this to affect him, he will only make Romeo more unhappy. He tries to leave but Benvolio insists on staying with him.
4 He asks who it is that Romeo loves.
5 Romeo avoids answering but tells Benvolio that she is beautiful ...

	Still-waking sleep, that is not what it is! 180
	This love feel I, that feel no love in this.
	Dost thou not laugh?
BENVOLIO	No coz, I rather weep.
ROMEO	Good heart, at what?
BENVOLIO	At thy good heart's oppression.
ROMEO	Why such is love's transgression.
	Griefs of mine own lie heavy in my breast,
	Which thou wilt propagate to have it pressed
	With more of thine. This love that thou hast shown
	Doth add more grief to too much of mine own.
	Love is a smoke made with the fume of sighs,
	Being purged, a fire sparkling in lovers' eyes, 190
	Being vexed, a sea nourished with lovers' tears,
	What is it else? A madness most discreet,
	A choking gall, and a preserving sweet.
	Farewell my coz.
BENVOLIO	Soft, I will go along.
	And if you leave me so, you do me wrong.
ROMEO	Tut I have lost myself; I am not here.
	This is not Romeo, he's some other where.
BENVOLIO	Tell me in sadness, who is that you love.
ROMEO	What, shall I groan and tell thee?
BENVOLIO	Groan? Why no.
	But sadly tell me who. 200
ROMEO	Bid a sick man in sadness make his will?
	A word ill urged to one that is so ill.
	In sadness cousin, I do love a woman.
BENVOLIO	I aimed so near, when I supposed you loved.
ROMEO	A right good mark-man. And she's fair I love.
BENVOLIO	A right fair mark, fair coz, is soonest hit.
ROMEO	Well in that hit you miss. She'll not be hit
	With Cupid's arrow. She hath Dian's wit,
	And in strong proof of chastity well armed, 209
	From love's weak childish bow she lives uncharmed.

Benvolio tells Romeo he should forget about her and look at other girls. Romeo says that is impossible. They leave.

6 ...and does not return his love. She has sworn that she will never marry.

7 Benvolio tries to persuade Romeo to forget about this girl. He should look at other pretty girls.

8 Romeo replies that this will just make him realise how beautiful she is. Benvolio will never persuade him to forget her.

9 Benvolio says that the will take that as a challenge.

6 ▷

7 ▷

8 ▷

9 ▷

	She will not stay the siege of loving terms,
	Nor bide th' encounter of assailing eyes,
	Nor ope her lap to saint-seducing gold.
	O she is rich in beauty, only poor,
	That when she dies, with beauty dies her store.
BENVOLIO	Then she hath sworn that she will still live chaste?
ROMEO	She hath, and in that sparing makes huge waste;

For beauty starved with her severity,
Cuts beauty off from all posterity.
She is too fair, too wise; wisely too fair,   220
To merit bliss by making me despair.
She hath forsworn to love, and in that vow
Do I live dead that live to tell it now.

BENVOLIO   Be ruled by me, forget to think of her.

ROMEO   O teach me how I should forget to think.

BENVOLIO   By giving liberty unto thine eyes.
Examine other beauties.

ROMEO   'Tis the way
To call hers, exquisite, in question more.
These happy masks that kiss fair ladies' brows,
Being black, put us in mind they hide the fair.   230
He that is strucken blind cannot forget
The precious treasure of his eyesight lost.
Show me a mistress that is passing fair,
What doth her beauty serve, but as a note
Where I may read who passed that passing fair?
Farewell, thou canst not teach me to forget.

BENVOLIO   I'll pay that doctrine, or else die in debt.

                                                                    [*Exeunt*

ACTIVITIES

Keeping track

Prologue

1 What do we find out about the play from this speech?
2 Why do you think Shakespeare starts the play in this way?

Scene 1

3 Why does the fighting start?
4 What is the reaction of each of these people to the fighting?
Benvolio, Tybalt, Capulet, Lady Capulet, Montague, Lady Montague.
5 What does the Prince do about the fighting?
6 What do we learn about Romeo from this scene?

Discussion

Scene 1 is dominated by the conflict between two great families, the Montagues and the Capulets. Look back over the Prologue and Scene 1.

1 How do you think it might have started?
2 Is it the fault more of one family than of the other? (If so, which?)
3 Could Prince Escalus have done more to try to stop it? (If so, what?)

Drama

'Three civil brawls bred of an airy word.'

Within 80 lines of the beginning of the play Shakespeare has filled the stage with 10 people speaking, a crowd, some courtiers and three fights. This would provide considerable problems for a director and actors. Together groups are going to plan the movements of the actors between lines 31 and 85.

1 The class divides into 5 groups, A-E.
2 Each group deals with a different set of people:
   Group A
   Samson, Gregory, Abraham, serving man, Benvolio.
   Start at line 33
   Group B
   Benvolio, Tybalt
   Start at line 64
   Group C
   Capulet, his wife, Montague, his wife.
   Start at line 73
   Group D
   citizens
   Start at line 71
   Group E
   Prince and his courtiers
   Start at line 79
3 Discuss how you think your group's characters behave:
   ● What are the main actions?
   ● What are the movements of the characters who speak?
   ● What are the movements of the characters who do
     not speak?
4 Write notes, or draw a diagram, to show the main moves.
5 Work the moves out in slow motion or create tableaux
   (see page 263).
6 As you work, discuss what you are doing. Take time to

think about it and change things as necessary.

Remember this is meant to be an exciting and tumultuous opening that would have the audience on the edge of their seats.

Characters

1 In this section of the play we meet one of the two main characters, Romeo. What are your first impressions of him:
   ● from what other people say about him
   ● from what he says (and the way he says it)
   ● from what he does?

2 Start Character logs (see page 260) for the main characters in Scene 1. You may find these lines helpful to start you off:

Tybalt	68-70, 110
Benvolio	62-3
Capulet	76-7
Lady Capulet	75
Montague	78, 157-8
Romeo	160, 205, 225, 236

Close study: Prologue

1 The Prologue can be divided into three sections:
   a   lines 1-4
   b   lines 5-8
   c   lines 9-14

   Each section is about a different topic. Write one sentence for each, summing up what it is about.

2 As well as outlining the **story** of the play, the Prologue introduces some of the main **themes**. Find as many words and phrases as you can connected with:
   ● fate
   ● death

3 When you are speaking Shakespeare's verse it is

important to decide where to pause. Sometimes you
should pause at the end of the line; at other times the
meaning of the sentence requires you not to. Which lines in
the prologue need a pause at the end, and which do not?
4 Practise reading the Prologue aloud. Concentrate on
getting the **meaning** across. Don't emphasise the **rhyme** or
rhythm - leave them to look after themselves!

Writing

Benvolio asks Romeo's father whether he has questioned his
son about his behaviour. Montague says that he has both
questioned Romeo himself and also persuaded friends to do
so. Write two short conversations that Montague has:
● with Romeo in which he tries to find out what is wrong
  with his son.
● with a family friend to whom he explains the situation and
  whom he asks to help.

Quiz

1 Is each of these a Capulet, or a Montague?
  Romeo, Tybalt, Abram, Sampson, Benvolio.
2 Why does Benvolio draw his sword?
3 Who says, and to whom?
  ● A crutch, a crutch! Why call you for a sword?
  ● Throw your mistempered weapons to the ground.
  ● Ay me! Sad hours seem long.
  ● I serve as good a man as you.
  ● … o brawling love, o loving hate …
  ● This love feel I, that feel no love in this.

Capulet talks to Paris, a wealthy young man of Verona, about his daughter Juliet. Paris is asking for Juliet's hand in marriage and although Capulet is not unwilling, he thinks Juliet is too young; Paris should wait another 2 years. Paris is unhappy at this, so Capulet agrees that he should woo his daughter; if she if willing, then they will talk again. He invites Paris to the feast he is giving that evening; he will meet Juliet then.

bound: (to keep the peace)
in penalty alike: under threat of the same punishment (death)
of honourable reckoning: of good reputation
lived at odds: lived as enemies
my suit: Paris has asked Capulet if he can marry Juliet.
saying o'er: repeating
is yet ... world: has lived a sheltered life
she hath not ... years: she is still only 14
marred: spoiled
ere: before
Earth ... she: all Capulet's other children have died.
she agreed: if she agrees.
within her scope ... voice: I will give my consent to her marrying the man she chooses.

1 Capulet tells Paris that he is holding a feast, as he does every Spring, for a large number of guests. He invites Paris and points out that he will meet many pretty girls there. He sends the servant out with a written list to

SCENE 2

Enter CAPULET, PARIS, *and* PETER

CAPULET   But Montague is bound as well as I,
In penalty alike; and 'tis not hard, I think,
For men so old as we to keep the peace.

PARIS   Of honourable reckoning are you both,
And pity 'tis lived at odds so long.
But now my lord, what say you to my suit?

CAPULET   But saying o'er what I have said before.
My child is yet a stranger in the world,
She hath not seen the change of fourteen years.
Let two more summers wither in their pride   10
Ere we may think her ripe to be a bride.

PARIS   Younger than she are happy mothers made.

CAPULET   And too soon marred are those so early made.
Earth hath swallowed all my hopes but she,
She is the hopeful lady of my earth.
But woo her gentle Paris, get her heart,
My will to her consent is but a part.
And she agreed, within her scope of choice
Lies my consent and fair according voice.
This night I hold an old accustomed feast,   20
Whereto I have invited many a guest,
Such as I love; and you among the store,
One more, most welcome, makes my number
    more.
At my poor house look to behold this night
Earth-treading stars that make dark heaven light.
Such comfort as do lusty young men feel,
When well-apparelled April on the heel

invite the guests.

The servant is sent off with a list of guests to invite, but he can't read. Benvolio and Romeo return.

2 The servant, speaking alone, tells us that he can't read.

one fire … anguish: one fire will put another one out (by burning up all the fuel), the pain will help you forget a previous one. (Benvolio is still trying to persuade Romeo that falling in love with another girl will help him forget his first love.)

holp: helped

plantain leaf: herbal remedy for cuts and grazes (Romeo is scorning Benvolio's help).

bound: Romeo feels that love has tied him up just as, in those days, people thought to be mad were tied up.

Godden: Good evening (but a greeting that could be used any time after noon). Also sometimes written as 'good den'.

Of limping winter treads, even such delight
Along fresh female buds shall you this night
Inherit at my house. Hear all, all see,　　　　30
And like her most whose merit most shall be;
Which on more view of, many—mine being one—
May stand in number, though in reckoning none.
Come go with me.—
[*To Peter, giving a paper*] Go sirrah, trudge about
Through fair Verona, find those persons out
Whose names are written there, and to them say,
My house and welcome on their pleasure stay.　37
　　　　　　　　　　　[*Exeunt Capulet and Paris*

PETER　　　　Find them out whose names are written here! It
is written that the shoemaker should meddle
with his yard, and the tailor with his last, the　40
fisher with his pencil, and the painter with his
nets. But I am sent to find those persons whose
names are here writ, and can never find what
names the writing person hath here writ. I must
to the learned, in good time.

Enter BENVOLIO *and* ROMEO

BENVOLIO　　Tut man, one fire burns out another's burning,
One pain is lessened by another's anguish;
Turn giddy, and be holp by backward turning;
One desperate grief cures with another's languish.
Take thou some new infection to thy eye,　　50
And the rank poison of the old will die.

ROMEO　　　Your plantain leaf is excellent for that.

BENVOLIO　　For what I pray thee?

ROMEO　　　　　　　　　　　　For your broken shin.

BENVOLIO　　Why Romeo, art thou mad?

ROMEO　　　Not mad, but bound more than a madman is;
Shut up in prison, kept without my food,
Whipped and tormented, and—Godden good fellow.

PETER　　　God gi' god-den. I pray sir can you read?

Benvolio and Romeo meet the servant, who asks
them to read the list for him. Romeo reads it aloud. It
includes the name of Rosaline, with whom he is in
love. He asks where the feast will take place. The
servant tells them that the feast is at the Capulets'
house. Benvolio tells Romeo that he should attend.
Then he will be able to compare Rosaline, whom he
loves, with other more beautiful girls and realise his
mistake.

Whither: to what place

crush: drink

ancient: long-established

the fair Rosaline: clearly Romeo has told Benvolio her
name after all.

Go thither: Go there

with unattainted eye: without prejudice

When the devout ... liars: Heretics were people who held
false beliefs and during the 16th century they were
sometimes punished for their beliefs, and even executed
by burning. Romeo sees his love as a religion. He says
that when his faith accepts something so false then may
his tears of love turn to fire and burn his eyes. Then, too,
may people who failed the test of faith (being tied up and
thrown into deep water) be burned as liars!

ROMEO	Ay, mine own fortune in my misery.
PETER	Perhaps you have learned it without book. But I pray can you read anything you see? 61
ROMEO	Ay, if I know the letters and the language.
PETER	Ye say honestly; rest you merry.
ROMEO	Stay fellow, I can read. [*Reads the paper*
	'Signior Martino, and his wife and daughters;
	County Anselme, and his beauteous sisters; the
	lady widow of Vitruvio; Signior Placentio, and
	his lovely nieces; Mercutio, and his brother
	Valentiine; mine uncle Capulet, his wife, and
	daughters; my fair niece Rosaline, and Livia; 70
	Signior Valentio, and his cousin Tybalt; Lucio,
	and the lively Helena.'
	A fair assembly. Whither should they come?
PETER	Up.
ROMEO	Whither? To supper?
PETER	To our house.
ROMEO	Whose house?
PETER	My master's.
ROMEO	Indeed I should have asked you that before.
PETER	Now I'll tell you without asking. My master is 80 the great rich Capulet; and if you be not of the house of Montagues, I pray come and crush a cup of wine. Rest you merry. [*Exit*
BENVOLIO	At this same ancient feast of Capulet's
	Sups the fair Rosaline whom thou so lov'st,
	With all the admired beauties of Verona.
	Go thither, and with unattainted eye,
	Compare her face with some that I shall show,
	And I will make thee think thy swan a crow.
ROMEO	When the devout religion of mine eye 90
	Maintains such falsehood, then turn tears to fires,
	And these who often drowned could never die,
	Transparent heretics, be burnt for liars.

Romeo disagrees strongly with this but says he will attend the feast to prove Benvolio wrong.

you saw her ... eye: You only thought she was beautiful because there was no one to compare her with.
shall scant show well: won't look so good

At the Capulets' house Lady Capulet tells Juliet's Nurse to call Juliet. Juliet comes. Lady Capulet and the Nurse discuss how old Juliet is: not quite fourteen.

1 ▷

1 Lady Capulet tells the Nurse to call Juliet. She does so.
2 Juliet arrives and asks her mother why she has called her. Lady Capulet first tells the Nurse to leave them and then calls her back; she, too, must be part of the conversation.

2 ▷

3 She confirms with the Nurse that Juliet is not yet fourteen.

3 ▷

One fairer than my love? The all-seeing sun
 Ne'er saw her match since first the world begun.

BENVOLIO Tut you saw her fair, none else being by,
Herself poised with herself in either eye.
But in that crystal scales let there be weighed
Your lady's love against some other maid
That I will show you shining at this feast,
And she shall scant show well that now seems best. 100

ROMEO I'll go along, no such sight to be shown,
But to rejoice in spendour of mine own. [*Exeunt*

SCENE **3**

A room in Capulet's mansion
Enter LADY CAPULET *and* NURSE

L. CAPULET Nurse, where's my daughter? Call her forth to me.
NURSE Now by my maidenhood–at twelve year old–
I bade her come. What lamb! What lady-bird!
God forbid! Where's this girl? What Juliet!

Enter JULIET

JULIET How now? Who calls?
NURSE Your mother.
JULIET Madam, I am here. What is your will?
L. CAPULET This is the matter–Nurse, give leave awhile,
We must talk in secret. Nurse, come back again,
I have remembered me, thou's hear our counsel.
Thou knowest my daughter's of a pretty age. 10
NURSE Faith I can tell her age unto an hour.
L. CAPULET She's not fourteen.
NURSE I'll lay fourteen of my teeth,
And yet to my teen be it spoken, I have but four,

The Nurse continues to recall events of Juliet's life when she was only two.

4 The nurse recalls Juliet's birth, on 31st July almost 14 years ago. She remembers, too, the occasion eleven years ago when Juliet was weaned. (The Nurse was engaged by the family to breastfeed the baby, a common practice in those days.)

5 She also remembers another event that happened at the same time: Juliet fell over and hurt herself. The Nurse's husband made a coarse remark and Juliet amused them all by agreeing with him, although she didn't, of course, understand what he meant.

She is not fourteen. How long is it now
To Lammas-tide?

L. CAPULET   A fortnight and odd days.

NURSE   Even or odd, of all days in the year,
Come Lammas Eve at night shall she be fourteen.
Susan and she–God rest all Christian souls–
Were of an age. Well, Susan is with God,
She was too good for me. But as I said,   20
On Lammas Eve at night shall she be fourteen;
That shall she, marry, I remember it well.
'Tis since the earthquake now eleven years,
And she was weaned–I never shall forget it–
Of all the days of the year, upon that day.
For I had then laid wormwood to my dug,
Sitting in the sun under the dove-house wall.
My lord and you were then at Mantua–
Nay I do bear a brain–but as I said,
When it did taste the wormwood on the nipple   30
Of my dug, and felt it bitter, pretty fool,
To see it tetchy and fall out with the dug.
'Shake,' quoth the dove-house; 'twas no need, I
    trow,
To bid me trudge.
And since that time it is eleven years,
For then she could stand high-lone; nay by the rood,
She could have run and waddled all about;
For even the day before, she broke her brow,
And then my husband–God be with his soul,
A' was a merry man–took up the child.   40
'Yea,' quoth he, 'dost thou fall upon thy face?
Thou wilt fall backward when thou hast more wit,
Wilt thou not Jule?' And by my holidame,
The pretty wretch left crying, and said 'Ay'.
To see how a jest shall come about! I warrant, an
I should live a thousand years,
I should never forget it. 'Wilt thou not Jule?'

Lady Capulet stops her, to ask Juliet how she would feel about the prospect of getting married. Lady Capulet reveals that Juliet has a suitor, Count Paris.

6 >

6 Lady Capulet tells the Nurse that that is quite enough, but the Nurse continues to chew over her story.

7 Juliet, too, begs her to stop.

8 The Nurse says that she has finished. She says Juliet was the prettiest baby she ever nursed and that her only wish now is to see Juliet married.

7 >
8 >

Were not I ... teat: If it weren't for the fact that I was the only nurse to feed you, I would say you took in your wisdom with the milk when you fed.

ladies of esteem: ladies from good families

a man of wax: like a waxwork, perfect

      quoth he,
      And pretty fool it stinted, and said 'Ay'.

L. CAPULET Enough of this, I prithee hold thy peace.

NURSE   Yes madam, yet I cannot choose but laugh,   50
      To think it should leave crying and say 'Ay'.
      And yet I warrant it had upon it brow
      A bump as big as a young cockerel's stone.
      A perilous knock, and it cried bitterly.
      'Yea' quoth my husband, 'fall'st upon thy face?
      Thou wilt fall backward when thou comest to age;
      Wilt thou not Jule?' It stinted, and said 'Ay'.

JULIET   And stint thou too, I pray thee Nurse, say I.

NURSE   Peace, I have done. God mark thee to his grace;
      Thou wast the prettiest babe that e'er I nursed. 60
      And I might live to see thee married once,
      I have my wish.

L. CAPULET Marry, that 'marry' is the very theme
      I came to talk of. Tell me daughter Juliet,
      How stands your dispositions to be married?

JULIET   It is an honour that I dream not of.

NURSE   An honour? Were not I thine only nurse,
      I would say thou hadst sucked wisdom from thy
        teat.

L. CAPULET Well, think of marriage now. Younger than you,
      Here in Verona, ladies of esteem,   70
      Are made already mothers. By my count,
      I was your mother much upon these years
      That you are now a maid. Thus then in brief
      The valiant Paris seeks you for his love.

NURSE   A man, young lady; lady, such a man
      As all the world – why he's a man of wax.

L. CAPULET Verona's summer hath not such a flower.

NURSE   Nay he's a flower, in faith a very flower.

L. CAPULET What say you, can you love the gentleman?
      This night you shall behold him at our feast. 80

She urges Juliet to meet him at the feast they are
holding that night. Juliet says she will do so. They
prepare to go to the feast.

---

writ: written

volume: Lady Capulet compares Paris to a book that Juliet
should read. This comparison (metaphor) is continued
over several lines.

married lineament: harmonious feature

one another lends content: they all fit together so
perfectly

And what obscured ... eyes: Find the things that are
hidden in the main part of the book written in the
margin (of his eyes).

this unbound lover: a play on words. He is like a book
that is incomplete, without a cover, and he is also, as a
lover free to do as he likes, because he is not married.

The fish ... story: These two sentences go together. Lady
Capulet describes Paris as the contents ('story') of the
book and Juliet as the cover ('golden clasps'). Just as the
sea provides a home for the fish that live in it, so the
handsome cover (Juliet) will provide a perfect home for
the book (Paris).

women grow by men: a play on words. By marriage
women grow in status, but they also grow in size by
becoming pregnant

look to like ... move: I'll look forward to liking him, if
looking at him can lead me to like him

But no more ... fly: But I won't allow my eye to get me
more involved (with him) than you would approve of.

1 A servant comes to tell Lady Capulet that the guests
have started to arrive. He asks them to come in to the
feast.

2 Lady Capulet says they are coming. She and the
Nurse tell Juliet to meet Paris and think of the future.

Read o'er the volume of young Paris' face,
And find delight writ there with beauty's pen;
Examine every married lineament,
And see how one another lends content;
And what obscured in this fair volume lies
Find written in the margent of his eyes.
This precious book of love, this unbound lover,
To beautify him only lacks a cover.
The fish lives in the sea, and 'tis much pride
For fair without the fair within to hide.   90
That book in many's eyes doth share the glory,
That in gold clasps locks in the golden story.
So shall you share all that he doth possess,
By having him, making yourself no less.

NURSE   No less, nay bigger; women grow by men.

L. CAPULET   Speak briefly; can you like of Paris' love?

JULIET   I'll look to like, if looking liking move.
But no more deep will I endart mine eye
Than your consent gives strength to make it fly.   99

Enter PETER *the Clown*

PETER   Madam, the guests are come, supper served up,
you called, my young lady asked for, the Nurse
cursed in the pantry, and every thing in
extremity. I must hence to wait; I beseech you
follow straight.

L. CAPULET   We follow thee. [*Exit Peter*] Juliet, the County
stays.

NURSE   Go girl, seek happy nights to happy days.
                                                  [*Exeunt*

ACTIVITIES

Keeping track

Scene 2

1 What age does Capulet want Juliet to be before she marries?
2 Why?
3 What is Benvolio talking about when he and Romeo reappear?
4 Why does Benvolio want Romeo to go to the Capulet's feast?

Scene 3

5 How old is Juliet?
6 Why does Lady Capulet include the Nurse in her conversation with Juliet?
7 How does Lady Capulet's attitude to marriage differ from her husband's?

Discussion

Romeo and love

Look again at Act 1 scene 1 lines 158-181 and Act 1 scene 2 lines 46-57 and 80-101.

1 What impression does Romeo give us about what it is like to be in love?
2 What does Benvolio suggest as a 'cure' for this?
3 What does this tell us about Benvolio's opinions of Romeo, and of love?

Love and marriage

Now look at the conversation between Juliet and her mother (Act 1 scene 3 lines 63-99).

4 In Lady Capulet's view what is the relationship between love and marriage? (For example, which does she think comes first in time? And in importance?)
5 What do you think of the different views of love expressed by Romeo, Benvolio, and Lady Capulet?

Drama

But as I said.

The nurse is a comic character who talks a lot . Work on her long speech in Scene 3 (lines 16 - 48).
Divide into groups of three and call yourselves A, B and C.
A: say the words as fast as you can read them - do not worry too much about understanding it all .
B and C: invent what Juliet and her mother would do all the way through this long speech.

Remember this is meant to be funny. Although the nurse is only a servant, the mother and daughter would be too well-mannered to interrupt an old lady, who has been with the family for at least fourteen years. Presumably they will also be used to her going on like this . They will be particularly exasperation because the question they asked only needed a brief answer.

Share your version with the rest of the class and see which is funniest. All groups could then try to reproduce that version. Are some people better at making others laugh? Why?

Character

1 Start Character logs for the new characters in these scenes. You may find it helpful to lock at these lines in Act 1 scene 3:

The Nurse   12-15, 59-62, 67-8, 106
Juliet   97-99

2 Add to your Character logs for:
   Capulet, Lady Capulet, Romeo, Benvolio

Close study

Act 1 scene 2 lines 83-100

1 Read Benvolio's first speech. What is the main point he is making?
2 What is Romeo's response?
3 In Benvolio's second speech, does he just say the same thing in different words, or does he say something new? If so, what?
4 Benvolio says a lot about beauty: he thinks it is important for a girl to be physically attractive. Pick out the words and phrases he uses that refer to beauty.
5 Romeo's reply concentrates on a different topic. What do these words and phrases tell us about how he views love?

   devout religion ... falsehood ... heretics ... liars ... since the world began
6 The first part of this section is in blank verse (see page 266). Then, at the end of Benvolio's first speech, it moves into rhyme. Note which lines rhyme. What effect does the rhyming have on this short section of the play?

Romeo, Mercutio, Benvolio, and their friends are on their way to the Capulets' ball.

1 Romeo asks whether they will make a formal speech to explain why they have arrived without being invited, or whether they will do without.

Writing

Before she goes to the feast, Juliet writes her diary,
describing what has happened so far that day, and her
thoughts about that, as well as what she feels about going
to the feast. Write her diary entry.

Quiz

1 All the quotations that follow are about **time**. Who says
   each, and to whom?
   ●   Younger than you,
      Here in Verona, ladies of esteem
      Are made already mothers.
   ● Younger than she are happy mothers made.
   ● She hath not seen the change of fourteen years.
2 Who:
   ●   cannot read?
   ● is Valentino's cousin?
   ● compares a young man to a book?
   ● was cursed in the pantry?
3 To what questions are these the answers (and who are
   the questioner and the person answering) ?
   ● A fortnight and odd days
   ● Up
   ● Ay, mine own fortune in my misery

SCENE **4**

A street outside Capulet's mansion
Enter ROMEO, MERCUTIO, BENVOLIO, *and* HORATIO,
with other Maskers and Torch-bearers

ROMEO   What, shall this speech be spoke for our excuse?
            Or shall we on without apology?
BENVOLIO   The date is out of such prolixity.
            We'll have no Cupid hoodwinked with a scarf,

Romeo is gloomy, partly because he is unhappily in love and because he is worried about how they will explain themselves: they haven't got invitations. Benvolio and Mercutio try to cheer him up, but with little success.

2 >

2 Benvolio answers that there is really no need for a formal speech (which was traditionally introduced by someone dressed as Cupid, blindfolded and carrying an imitation bow). Instead they should let people judge them for what they are.

3 >

3 Romeo replies that he will carry the torch while the others dance. He feels too heavy-hearted to dance.
4 He complains that love is rough and hurts those who fall in love.
5 Mercutio tells Romeo he should be rougher with love. He calls for his mask so that they can all go on to the ball.

4 >

6 Romeo again insists that he won't dance but will carry the light.

5 >

6 >

Bearing a Tartar's painted bow of lath,
Scaring the ladies like a crow-keeper;
Nor no without-book prologue, faintly spoke
After the prompter, for our entrance.
But let them measure us by what they will,
We'll measure them a measure, and be gone.   10

ROMEO   Give me a torch, I am not for this ambling.
             Being but heavy, I will bear the light.

MERCUTIO   Nay gentle Romeo, we must have you dance.

ROMEO   Not I, believe me, you have dancing shoes
             With nimble soles, I have a soul of lead
             So stakes me to the ground I cannot move.

MERCUTIO   You are a lover; borrow Cupid's wings,
             And soar with them above a common bound.

ROMEO   I am too sore empierced with his shaft,
             To soar with his light feathers; and so bound,   20
             I cannot bound a pitch above dull woe.
             Under love's heavy burden do I sink.

MERCUTIO   And to sink in it should you burden love;
             Too great oppression for a tender thing.

ROMEO   Is love a tender thing? It is too rough,
             Too rude, too boisterous, and it pricks like thorn.

MERCUTIO   If love be rough with you, be rough with love.
             Prick love for pricking, and you beat love down.
             Give me a case to put my visage in.
             A visor for a visor. What care I   30
             What curious eye doth quote deformities?
             Here are the beetle brows shall blush for me.

BENVOLIO   Come knock and enter, and no sooner in,
             But every man betake him to his legs.

ROMEO   A torch for me; let wantons light of heart
             Tickle the senseless rushes with their heels.
             For I am proverbed with a grandsire phrase:
             I'll be a candle-holder and look on;
             The game was ne'er so fair, and I am done.

Mercutio continues to try to joke Romeo out of his
sombre mood. When Romeo mentions a dream,
Mercutio launches into a fanciful account of Queen
Mab who travels into people's dreams.

7 >

7 Mercutio makes fun of him.
8 When Romeo disagrees, Mercutio points out that they
  are wasting time.

8 >

9 Romeo tries to describe his dream, probably some
  kind of premonition, but Mercutio interrupts.

Queen Mab : the queen of the fairies
the fairies' midwife: just as a midwife helps deliver babies,
  so Queen Mab helps deliver dreams
agate: a precious stone used in signet rings, often engraved
  with a tiny picture

9 >

alderman: a senior local councillor
atomies: atoms
spinners: craneflies (or daddy-long-legs)
traces: the straps that connect the horse's harness to the
  wagon
collars: the horses' collars
a round little ... maid: people used to say that maggots
  would breed in the hands of girls who were lazy
joiner: someone who works in wood, making windows,
  doors etc

MERCUTIO	Tut, dun's the mouse, the constable's own word. 40
	If thou art Dun, we'll draw thee from the mire
	Of this save-your-reverence love, wherein thou stickest
	Up to the ears. Come, we burn daylight, ho!
ROMEO	Nay that's not so.
MERCUTIO	I mean sir, in delay
	We waste our lights in vain, like lights by day.
	Take our good meaning, for our judgment sits
	Five times in that, ere once in our five wits.
ROMEO	And we mean well in going to this mask;.
	But 'tis no wit to go.
MERCUTIO	Why, may one ask?
ROMEO	I dreamt a dream tonight.
MERCUTIO	And so did I. 50
ROMEO	Well, what was yours?
MERCUTIO	That dreamers often lie.
ROMEO	In bed asleep while they do dream things true.
MERCUTIO	O then I see Queen Mab hath been with you.
	She is the fairies' midwife, and she comes
	In shape no bigger than an agate stone
	On the fore-finger of an alderman,
	Drawn with a team of little atomies
	Over men's noses as they lie asleep.
	Her wagon-spokes made of long spinners' legs;
	The cover, of the wings of grasshoppers; 60
	Her traces, of the smallest spider web;
	Her collars, of the moonshine's watery beams;
	Her whip, of cricket's bone; the lash, of film;
	Her wagoner, a small gray-coated gnat,
	Not half so big as a round little worm
	Pricked from the lazy finger of a maid.
	Her chariot is an empty hazel-nut,
	Made by the joiner squirrel or old grub,
	Time out a mind the fairies' coachmakers.

Mercutio describes how Queen Mab leads people to dream of what they most desire - although this only shows their least attractive side.

courtiers: people who spent time at the royal court, often trying to gain money, titles or power for themselves.

curtsies: courtiers would have to show 'courtesies', marks of politeness, to the king or queen when at court

straight: immediately

sweetmeats: eaten to make the breath smell sweet

smelling out a suit: courtiers made money by offering to put in a good word to the king or queen for someone who wanted a favour

tithe-pigs: the parson was entitled to one tenth (a tithe) of the income of everyone in the parish. So if your sow had a litter, the tenth piglet had to go to the parson.

parson: parish priest

benefice: the parson's living - the parish and the income he got from it

Of breaches ... fathom deep: of breaking down castle walls, of ambushes, of Spanish swords (the best), of drinks thirty feet deep.

bakes the elf-locks ... hairs: makes dirty hair into matted tangles

This is the hag ... carriage: people believed that if someone dreamed about lovemaking, the partner they dreamed of was really a devil or evil fairy

10 Romeo tries to interrupt Mercutio, but without much success, since by now Mercutio has really psyched himself up.

10

And in this state she gallops night by night   70
Through lovers' brains, and then they dream of
    love;
O'er courtiers' knees, that dream on curtsies
    straight;
O'er lawyers' fingers, who straight dream on fees;
O'er ladies' lips, who straight on kisses dream,
Which oft the angry Mab with blisters plagues,
Because their breaths with sweetmeats tainted are.
Sometime she gallops o'er a courtier's nose,
And then dreams he of smelling out a suit;
And sometime comes she with a tithe-pig's tail,
Tickling a parson's nose as 'a lies asleep,   80
Then he dreams of another benefice.
Sometimes she driveth o'er a soldier's neck,
And then dreams he of cutting foreign throats,
Of breaches, ambuscadoes, Spanish blades,
Of healths five fathom deep; and then anon
Drums in his ear, at which he starts and wakes;
And being thus frighted, swears a prayer or two,
And sleeps again. This is that very Mab
That plaits the manes of horses in the night,
And bakes the elf-locks in foul sluttish hairs,   90
Which one untangled much misfortune bodes.
This is the hag, when maids lie on their backs,
That presses them and learns them first to bear,
Making them women of good carriage.
This is she—

ROMEO   Peace, peace, Mercutio, peace.
Thou talk'st of nothing.

MERCUTIO   True, I talk of dreams;
Which are the children of an idle brain,
Begot of nothing but vain fantasy;
Which is as thin of substance as the air,
And more inconstant than the wind who woos   100
Even now the frozen bosom of the north,
And being angered puffs away from thence,

Benvolio points out that they are just wasting time.
Romeo speaks of his sense of foreboding about what is
to happen. They move on to the Capulets' house,
where dinner is over and the servants are preparing
for the masked dance.

11 Benvolio brings them back to earth by pointing out
    that they are still no nearer getting to the dance.

my mind misgives: I have a premonition
Some consequence ... death: Romeo believes that he has
    mortgaged his life in return for love. It is written in the
    stars that events that night will lead to his being asked to
    repay this debt with his life.

1 The servants clear up after the meal. Sampson bustles
   about complaining that one of the other servants,
   Potpan, isn't pulling his weight.
2 Gregory agrees that the other two servants aren't up to
   scratch.
3 Sampson rushes round shouting out orders (but he
   isn't too busy to ask for someone to save him a piece of
   marzipan and to let their girlfriends into the house -
   the servants are going to have their own party later
   on).
4 When Anthony and Potpan arrive, Sampson tells them
   off, but they tell him that they can't be everywhere at
   the same time.

	Turning his side to the dew-dropping south.
BENVOLIO	This wind you talk of blows us from ourselves.
	Supper is done, and we shall come too late.
ROMEO	I fear, too early; for my mind misgives
	Some consequence, yet hanging in the stars,
	Shall bitterly begin his fearful date
	With this night's revels, and expire the term
	Of a despised life closed in my breast,
	By some vile forfeit of untimely death.
	But he that hath the steerage of my course
	Direct my suit. On lusty gentlemen.
BENVOLIO	Strike drum.

110

SCENE 5

The Great Hall in Capulet's mansion
They march about the stage, and Servingmen come
forth with napkins

SAMPSON	Where's Potpan, that he helps not to take away?
	He shift a trencher? He scrape a trencher?
GREGORY	When good manners shall lie all in one or two
	men's hands, and they unwashed too, 'tis a foul
	thing.
SAMPSON	Away with the joint-stools, remove the court-
	cupboard, look to the plate. Good thou, save me
	a piece of marchpane, and as thou lovest me, let
	the porter let in Susan Grindstone and Nell.
	Anthony and Potpan!
ANTHONY	Ay boy, ready.
SAMPSON	You are looked for, and called for, asked for, and
	sought for in the great chamber.
POTPAN	We cannot be here and there too. Cheerly boys,
	be brisk awhile, and the longer liver take all.

10

Capulet welcomes his guests to the ball and encourages them to dance. Some of the ladies are a bit shy and Capulet teases them that if they don't dance people will think they've got corns on their feet. He tells the musicians to play and the servants to clear the tables out of the way. Then he and an elderly relative sit watching the dancers and reminisce about the last time the two of them danced like this. Romeo catches sight of Juliet.

unplagued: untroubled
walk a bout: have a dance
makes dainty: is shy
Am I come ... now: have I got to the truth of it now?
visor: mask
A hall, a hall: clear a space for the dance
turn the tables up: move the tables out of the way
unlooked for: unexpected
nuptial: wedding
Pentecost: the Christian festival of Whitsun, fifty days after Easter
but a ward: not yet an adult

Enter CAPULET, LADY CAPULET, JULIET, TYBALT,
and all the Guests and Gentlewomen to the Maskers

CAPULET   Welcome gentlemen. Ladies that have their toes
Unplagued with corns will walk a bout with you.
Ah ha, my mistresses, which of you all
Will now deny to dance? She that makes dainty,
She I'll swear hath corns. Am I come near ye now? 20
Welcome gentlemen. I have seen the day
That I have worn a visor and could tell
A whispering tale in a fair lady's ear,
Such as would please. 'Tis gone, 'tis gone, 'tis gone.
You are welcome, gentlemen. Come, musicians
   play.
A hall, a hall, give room, and foot it girls.
                              [*Music plays, and they dance*
More light you knaves, and turn the tables up;
And quench the fire, the room is grown too hot.
Ah sirrah, this unlooked-for sport comes well.
Nay sit, nay sit, good cousin Capulet,   30
For you and I are past our dancing days.
How long is 't now since last yourself and I
Were in a mask?

2ND CAPULET   By'r lady, thirty years.

CAPULET   What man, 'tis not so much, 'tis not so much.
'Tis since the nuptial of Lucentio,
Come Pentecost as quickly as it will,
Some five and twenty years, and then we masked.

2ND CAPULET 'Tis more, 'tis more, his son is elder sir;
His son is thirty.

CAPULET   Will you tell me that?
His son was but a ward two years ago.   40

ROMEO   [*To a Servingman*] What lady's that which doth
   enrich the hand
Of yonder knight?

SERVINGMAN   I know not sir.

Romeo is stunned by Juliet's beauty. Tybalt sees Romeo and recognises him as a Montague. He becomes very angry but Capulet orders him to do nothing.

Ethiop: a black African

So shows ... rude hand: that lady stands out from the others like a white dove among black crows. When the dance is over, I'll watch where she goes and then, by touching her hand, bless my own rough hand.

Forswear: deny

Fetch me ...: Tybalt tells his page to get his sword

slave: a term of abuse

antic face: weird mask

fleer: make fun

solemnity: festivities

by the stock ... kin: by the ancestors and honour of my family

'A bears him ... gentleman: he behaves himself like a well-mannered person from a good family

well governed: well-behaved

do him disparagement: insult him

take no note: leave him alone

It is my will ... feast: This is what I want and if you respect me you will put a good face on things and not scowl, because such behaviour is totally unsuitable for a celebration

It fits: It is suitable

endure: put up with

ROMEO	O she doth teach the torches to burn bright.
	It seems she hangs upon the cheek of night
	Like a rich jewel in an Ethiop's ear;
	Beauty too rich for use, for earth too dear.
	So shows a snowy dove trooping with crows,
	As yonder lady o'er her fellows shows.
	The measure done, I'll watch her place of stand,
	And touching hers make blessed my rude hand. 50
	Did my heart love till now? Forswear it sight,
	For I ne'er saw true beauty till this night.
TYBALT	This by his voice should be a Montague.
	Fetch me my rapier, boy. What dares the slave
	Come hither, covered with an antic face,
	To fleer and scorn at our solemnity?
	Now by the stock and honour of my kin,
	To strike him dead I hold it not a sin.
CAPULET	Why how now kinsman, wherefore storm you so?
TYBALT	Uncle, this is a Montague, our foe; 60
	A villain that is hither come in spite,
	To scorn at our solemnity this night.
CAPULET	Young Romeo is it?
TYBALT	'Tis he, that villain Romeo.
CAPULET	Content thee gentle coz, let him alone.
	'A bears him like a portly gentleman;
	And to say truth, Verona brags of him
	To be a virtuous and well governed youth.
	I would not for the wealth of all this town
	Here in my house do him disparagement.
	Therefore be patient, take no note of him; 70
	It is my will, the which if thou respect,
	Show a fair presence, and put off these frowns,
	An ill-beseeming semblance for a feast.
TYBALT	It fits when such a villain is a guest.
	I'll not endure him.
CAPULET	He shall be endured.

Tybalt protests but Capulet is firm. Tybalt leaves, muttering that he will not forget what has happened. Romeo approaches Juliet and speaks to her for the first time.

goodman boy: a deliberate insult, putting Tybalt in his place

Go to: an expression of anger

You'll make ... be the man: You want to cause a disturbance amongst my guests? You want to stir it all up? You'd be a really big boy then, wouldn't you?

saucy: (stronger in Shakespeare's day) insolent

This trick ... scathe you: If you go on like this, you'll suffer for it.

contrary: contradict

princox: insolent boy

Patience perforce ... bitterest gall: I'm forced to be patient, but inside I'm boiling with rage and this mixture of feelings makes me tremble. I'll go away (and calm down) but although my mood may seem sweet now, it will turn into bitter hatred.

profane/shrine/pilgrim: Romeo speaks of Juliet's hand as the shrine to which pilgrims (his lips) travel to worship (kiss). Even touching the shrine may defile it, but then his lips will remedy this.

mannerly: well-behaved

palm to palm ... kiss: pilgrims returning from the Holy Land carried a palm and so were called palmers. A more suitable greeting ('kiss') for a palmer would be to touch hands ('palms')

Saints do not move: Juliet is thinking of the statue of the saint at the shrine.

What goodman boy, I say he shall; Go to,
Am I the master here or you? Go to.
You'll not endure him? God shall mend my soul,
You'll make a mutiny among my guests?
You will set cock-a-hoop, you'll be the man? 80

TYBALT   Why, uncle, 'tis a shame—

CAPULET   Go to, go to,
You are a saucy boy. Is 't so indeed?
This trick may chance to scathe you I know what.
You must contrary me? Marry 'tis time.
[*To Guests*] Well said my hearts! [*To Tybalt*] You
    are a princox, go;
Be quiet, or—[*To Servants*] More light, more
    light! [*To Tybalt*]For shame!
I'll make you quiet. [*To Guests*] What, cheerly
    my hearts!

TYBALT   Patience perforce with wilful choler meeting
Makes my flesh tremble in their different greeting.
I will withdraw, but this intrusion shall,   90
Now seeming sweet, convert to bitterest gall.
                                    [*Exit*

ROMEO   [*To Juliet*] If I profane with my unworthiest hand
This holy shrine, the gentle sin is this,
My lips two blushing pilgrims ready stand
To smooth that rough touch with a tender kiss.

JULIET   Good pilgrim, you do wrong your hand too much,
Which mannerly devotion shows in this;
For saints have hands that pilgrims' hands do touch,
And palm to palm is holy palmers' kiss.

ROMEO   Have not saints lips, and holy palmers too?   100

JULIET   Ay pilgrim lips that they must use in prayer.

ROMEO   O then dear saint, let lips do what hands do.
They pray; grant thou, lest faith turn to despair.

JULIET   Saints do not move, though grant for prayers' sake.

**They kiss. The Nurse interrupts with a message that
Juliet's mother wishes to speak to her. Romeo asks
the Nurse who Juliet is and learns that she is a
Capulet. The guests begin to leave.**

prayer's effect: the kiss
purged: cleansed
by th'book: expertly
have the chinks: get the cash, be in the money
my life ... debt: my life now depends on my enemy
Away be gone ... best: Let's leave now while things are
    still going really well.
Ay, so I ... unrest: Romeo agrees; things have gone 'well'
    for him, but he is dismayed at what will happen in the
    future because of his new love for Juliet.
banquet: light refreshments
They whisper ...: The guests excuse themselves. We have
    to guess what they say, from Capulet's reply.
waxes: grows
yond: over there

ROMEO   Then move not, while my prayer's effect I take.

                              [Kisses her

            Thus from my lips, by thine, my sin is purged.

JULIET   Then have my lips the sin that they have took.

ROMEO   Sin from my lips? O trespass sweetly urged.

            Give me my sin again.

JULIET   You kiss by th' book.

NURSE   Madam your mother craves a word with you.   110

ROMEO   What is her mother?

NURSE   Marry bachelor,

            Her mother is the lady of the house,

            And a good lady, and a wise and virtuous.

            I nursed her daughter that you talked withal.

            I tell you, he that can lay hold of her

            Shall have the chinks.

ROMEO   Is she a Capulet?

            O dear account, my life is my foe's debt.

BENVOLIO   Away, be gone, the sport is at the best.

ROMEO   Ay, so I fear, the more is my unrest.

CAPULET   Nay gentlemen, prepare not to be gone;   120

            We have a trifling foolish banquet towards.

                    [They whisper in his ear

            Is it e'en so? Why then I thank you all.

            I thank you honest gentlemen; good night.

            More torches here! Come on then, let's to bed.

            Ah sirrah, by my fay, it waxes late.

            I'll to my rest.

                           [Exeunt

JULIET   Come hither Nurse. What is yond gentleman?

NURSE   The son and heir of old Tiberio.

JULIET   What's he that now is going out of door?

NURSE   Marry that I think be young Petruchio.   130

JULIET   What's he that follows here that would not dance?

                              [Exit Romeo

Juliet sends her Nurse to discover Romeo's name. She is dismayed to learn that he is a Montague. Then they, too, leave.

My grave ... bed: I'll die unmarried (or I'll die if I can't marry him).

Too early seen ... late: I saw Romeo and fell in love with him before I knew who he was. Now I do know who he is, it's too late for me to change my feelings.

Prodigious: monstrous

withal: recently

ACTIVITIES

Keeping track

1 How would you describe the mood of each of these characters as they go to the Capulets' ball? Mercutio, Benvolio, Romeo

2 What is Romeo's first reaction when he sees Juliet?

3 What makes Tybalt so angry?

4 Why does Capulet lose his temper with Tybalt?

5 How does Romeo feel when he learns that Juliet is a Capulet?

NURSE	I know not.
JULIET	Go ask his name – If he be married, My grave is like to be my wedding-bed.
NURSE	His name is Romeo, and a Montague, The only son of your great enemy.
JULIET	My only love sprung from my only hate, Too early seen unknown, and known too late! Prodigious birth of love it is to me, That I must love a loathed enemy. 140
NURSE	What 's tis, what 's tis?
JULIET	A rhyme I learned even now Of one I danced withal. [*One calls within ' Juliet!'*]
NURSE	Anon, anon! Come let's away, the strangers all are gone. [*Exeunt*

Discussion

Approval and disapproval

- In this scene there are many occasions on which one
  character expresses disapproval of another. Find them
  and make a list of the characters who speak and the
  characters they are talking about. Write down the words
  that are used.
- There are also occasions when characters express strong
  approval of others. Do the same for these.
- Now use the words and phrases you have collected to
  make an 'attitude poster' Take a large sheet of paper;
  draw the characters you have listed (or write their names)

and arrange your words and phrases on it so that it is
clear who is saying what about whom.

Love, hate and fate

These three important themes from the play are strongly
present in this scene. Work on them in a group of three
or four.

- Find all the occasions when characters refer to any of
  the themes.
- Make a list of key quotations illustrating each theme.
  In particular, look for images which express the
  themes vividly. (For example when Tybalt says 'this
  intrusion shall, Now seeming sweet, convert to
  bitterest gall' he makes us taste his hatred.)
- Now look at the quotations you have collected.
  Prepare a group reading in which you present them to
  the rest of the class. Decide on the best order for them
  - to show the contrasts and similarities between the
  lines you have selected. (You may decide to add extra
  lines to help with this.) Divide the lines between you
  and practise your reading.

Drama

'Across a crowded room''

'O , she doth teach the torches to burn bright'
Whole class activity.
One could imagine that this is the moment when Romeo
and Juliet see each other and fall in love. It could be
possible that Tybalt sees it at the same moment. In fact
all the fate, love and hate of the play could be captured in
this moment of time.
Using Forum Theatre techniques (see page 264) explore
this moment paying particular attention to the position,
gesture and facial expression of the three main
characters.

Follow up work.

If you have time you could add the other characters who are present at the masque and demonstrate whether they are aware of what is going on or not.

Character

Capulet and Tybalt

This is the second time we have met these two characters. Compare the way they behave here with their behaviour in Act 1 scene 1. In what ways is it similar? and different? Make notes in your Character log.

Romeo

Although this is a very important scene, Romeo actually says very little. Look carefully at what he says and does. Compare it with his behaviour in Act 1 scene 1 (especially lines 169-236). Is he the same? Has he changed? If so, how? Make notes in your Character log.

Juliet

Look especially at the way in which Juliet reacts to Romeo's advances. What does this tell us about:
● her intelligence
● her sense of humour?
How does she react when she discovers who Romeo is? Compare this with what Romeo says when he discovers who Juliet is. Make notes in your Character log.

Close study

Lines 90-109

Read this section of the scene carefully. Mark the sections that you do not fully understand. Use a dictionary if there are any words you are not sure about.

Language

- Make a list of all the 'religious' words used. Why do you think there are so many?
- Romeo takes the lead in this conversation. In Shakespeare's day this would be expected. But does it mean that Romeo behaves in a dominant or macho way? How does he see himself?
- The conversation is like a board game: first Romeo makes a move and then Juliet counters it. At the beginning does she want him to kiss her? Has she changed by the end? Why does the conversation take this form?

Verse form

These fourteen lines are in the form of a sonnet, a popular verse form in Shakespeare's day.

- How do they rhyme?
- Do the lines group together in any particular way?
- What is the effect of putting the lovers' first meeting into this special form?

Writing

1 Juliet keeps a personal diary in which she records not only the events of each day but also her secret thoughts and feelings about them. Write her diary entry for this day.

2 Leaving the ball, Tybalt meets an old friend. They go off and drink together. Tybalt tells his friend about what has happened. Write their conversation, either as a script, or as a story (using direct speech).

3 When the guests have gone, Capulet and his wife discuss the feast. Write their conversation, either as a script, or as a story (using direct speech).

4 You are the gossip writer of the *Verona Gazette*. You have been at the feast and have seen quite a lot of what has gone on (but not everything, so you have to

do some guesswork). Write your column for the next day.

Writing about Act 1

Take this opportunity to look back over the whole act. A number of key themes are introduced:

- Youth and age
- Love
- Hatred, aggression and justice
- Fate

Choose one of these and make a list of the occasions when
- people talk about it, directly or indirectly
- people's actions tell you something about it
- the language of the play contains images that refer to it.

Use your notes as the basis for one or two paragraphs (100-150 words) about your chosen theme.

The Chorus sums up what has happened in Act one and what will happen in Act two.

Romeo is on his way home, but turns back to the Capulets' house again. Benvolio and Mercutio are looking for him but do not see him. Benvolio realises that Romeo has climbed the wall into the grounds of the Capulets' house.

1 Romeo realises that he is so much in love with Juliet he must go back and try to find her.
2 Benvolio and Mercutio arrive, looking for Romeo. Mercutio says Romeo has gone home to bed.
3 Benvolio says that he has climbed the orchard wall (into the Capulets' grounds).

1 >

2 >

3 >

Act two

Outside Capulet's house
Enter CHORUS

CHORUS   Now old desire doth in his death-bed lie,
And young affection gapes to be his heir.
That fair for which love groaned for and would die,
With tender Juliet matched, is now not fair.
Now Romeo is beloved and loves again,
Alike bewitched by the charm of looks;
But to his foe supposed he must complain,
And she steals love's sweet bait from fearful hooks.
Being held a foe, he may not have access
To breathe such vows as lovers use to swear;   10
And she as much in love, her means much less
To meet her new-beloved any where.
But passion lends them power, time means, to
    meet,
Temp'ring extremities with extreme sweet. [*Exit*

SCENE 1

Enter ROMEO *alone*

ROMEO   Can I go forward when my heart is here?
Turn back, dull earth, and find thy centre out.

Enter BENVOLIO *and* MERCUTIO

BENVOLIO   Romeo! My cousin Romeo! Romeo!
MERCUTIO   He is wise,
And on my life hath stolen him home to bed.
BENVOLIO   He ran this way and leaped this orchard wall.
Call, good Mercutio.
MERCUTIO   Nay I'll conjure too.

Mercutio calls after him various taunting and bawdy remarks, but, getting no response, the two of them continue on their way home.

4

4 Mercutio pretends to 'conjure' Romeo (as a Magician conjures up a spirit) and does so in words that will certainly anger Romeo if he can hear them.

5 Benvolio points this out, but Mercutio continues in the same way.

6 Benvolio tells Mercutio that Romeo is hiding in the trees, because of love, so they might as well go home.

7 Mercutio continues to taunt the hidden Romeo in language that is increasingly obscene.

5

6

7

Romeo! Humours! Madman! Passion! Lover!
Appear thou in the likeness of a sigh,
Speak but one rhyme, and I am satisfied;
Cry but 'Ay me,' pronounce but 'love' and
    'dove';   10
Speak to my gossip Venus one fair word,
One nickname for her purblind son and heir,
Young Abraham Cupid, he that shot so trim,
When King Cophetua loved the beggar-maid.
He heareth not, he stirreth not, he moveth not;
The ape is dead, and I must conjure him.
I conjure thee by Rosaline's bright eyes,
By her high forehead, and her scarlet lip,
By her fine foot, straight leg, and quivering thigh,
And the demesnes that there adjacent lie,   20
That in thy likeness thou appear to us.

BENVOLIO   And if he hear thee, thou wilt anger him.

MERCUTIO   This cannot anger him; 'twould anger him
To raise a spirit in his mistress' circle
Of some strange nature, letting it there stand
Till she had laid it and conjured it down;
That were some spite. My invocation
Is fair and honest; in his mistress' name,
I conjure only but to raise up him.

BENVOLIO   Come, he hath hid himself among these trees 30
To be consorted with the humorous night.
Blind is his love, and best befits the dark.

MERCUTIO   If love be blind, love cannot hit the mark.
Now will he sit under a medlar tree,
And wish his mistress were that kind of fruit
As maids call medlars, when they laugh alone,
O Romeo that she were, O that she were
An open-arse and thou a poperin pear.
Romeo good night, I'll to my truckle-bed;
This field-bed is too cold for me to sleep.   40
Come, shall we go?

8 Since there is still no response from Romeo, the two of them agree to go home to bed.

8 ▷

Benvolio and Mercutio leave. Romeo is in the garden of the Capulets' house. In the moonlight he sees Juliet at an upstairs window.

jests at scars: makes fun of injuries (inflicted by being in love)

But soft ... breaks: Romeo sees Juliet at an upper window. She seems so bright to him that he compares her to the sun

moon: The house and garden are lit by the moon. In Classical mythology Diana, the goddess of the moon was served by virgins who wore a costume (vestal livery) that was pale in colour like the moonlight (sick and green). Romeo says that the moon is jealous of her maid Juliet because she is more beautiful. He encourages her to stop serving Diana, and so stop being a virgin and become his lover.

discourses: speaks

spheres: in classical times people believed that the stars and planets were fixed in transparent spheres that moved around the earth.

What if ... head: How would it be if her eyes were shining in the sky and in their place in her head there were two stars?

airy region: sky

BENVOLIO   Go then, for 'tis in vain
To seek him here that means not to be found.
[*Exeunt*

SCENE 2

Capulet's orchard

ROMEO   He jests at scars that never felt a wound.
But soft, what light through yonder window breaks?
It is the east, and Juliet is the sun.
Arise fair sun and kill the envious moon,
Who is already sick and pale with grief
That thou her maid art far more fair than she.
Be not her maid since she is envious.
Her vestal livery is but sick and green,
And none but fools do wear it; cast it off.

JULIET *appears at the window*

It is my lady, O it is my love.   10
O that she knew she were.
She speaks, yet she says nothing. What of that?
Her eye discourses, I will answer it.
I am too bold, 'tis not to me she speaks.
Two of the fairest stars in all the heaven
Having some business, do entreat her eyes
To twinkle in their spheres till they return.
What if her eyes were there, they in her head?
The brightness of her cheek would shame those
    stars,
As daylight doth a lamp; her eyes in heaven   20
Would through the airy region stream so bright
That birds would sing, and think it were not night.
See how she leans her cheek upon her hand.
O that I were a glove upon that hand,
That I might touch that cheek.

Juliet, thinking she is alone, speaks aloud of her love for Romeo and the problem that their family names cause them. But, she says, names are not important: it is the reality underneath that matters. To her surprise Romeo answers her and declares himself.

white upturned: looking upwards so that the whites show

wherefore ... Romeo: Why are you called Romeo (i.e. a Montague) and not some other name?

Thou art ... Montague: You would still be the same person, even if you were not called Montague

So Romeo ... that title: So Romeo would still be as perfect even if he were not called Romeo

owes: owns

doff: take off

bescreened : hidden

stumblest on my counsel: breaks in upon my secret thoughts (which she is saying out loud)

JULIET	Ay me!
ROMEO	She speaks.

O speak again, bright angel, for thou art
As glorious to this night, being o'er my head,
As is a winged messenger of heaven
Unto the white upturned, wond'ring eyes
Of mortals that fall back to gaze on him,   30
When he bestrides the lazy-passing clouds,
And sails upon the bosom of the air.

JULIET O Romeo, Romeo, wherefore art thou Romeo?
Deny thy father, and refuse thy name.
Or if thou wilt not, be but sworn my love,
And I'll no longer be a Capulet.

ROMEO [*Aside*] Shall I hear more, or shall I speak at this?

JULIET 'Tis but thy name that is my enemy.
Thou art thyself, though not a Montague.
What's Montague? It is nor hand nor foot,   40
Nor arm nor face, nor any other part
Belonging to a man. O be some other name.
What's in a name? That which we call a rose
By any other word would smell as sweet.
So Romeo would, were he not Romeo called,
Retain that dear perfection which he owes
Without that title. Romeo doff thy name,
And for that name which is no part of thee,
Take all myself.

ROMEO   I take thee at thy word.
Call me but 'love', and I'll be new baptized.   50
Henceforth I never will be Romeo.

JULIET What man art thou, that thus bescreened in night
So stumblest on my counsel?

ROMEO   By a name
I know not how to tell thee who I am.
My name, dear saint, is hateful to myself.
Because it is an enemy to thee.
Had I it written, I would tear the word.

**She asks how he got there. How did he find the way?
Love gave him the means, he replies.**

thee dislike: is unpleasant to you

wherefore: why

o'erperch: fly over

stony limits: boundary walls

dares love: love dares to

look thou but sweet: if you would only look favourably on me

My life ... thy love: I'd rather they killed me because of their hatred than go on living, waiting for death, without your love

counsel: advice

I am no pilot ... merchandise: I'm not a sailor but if you were living at the far side of the farthest ocean I would travel there to find you

Fain would ... form: I would much rather behave in a 'correct' formal way

farewell compliment: goodbye to formal behaviour

swearest: speak using flowery language and promises (as was fashionable among young men)

perjuries: lies

JULIET	My ears have not yet drunk a hundred words
	Of thy tongue's uttering, yet I know the sound.
	Art thou not Romeo, and a Montague? 60
ROMEO	Neither, fair maid, if either thee dislike.
JULIET	How cam'st thou hither, tell me, and wherefore?
	The orchard walls are high, and hard to climb,
	And the place death, considering who thou art,
	If any of my kinsmen find thee here.
ROMEO	With love's light wings did I o'erperch these walls,
	For stony limits cannot hold love out,
	And what love can do, that dares love attempt.
	Therefore thy kinsmen are no stop to me.
JULIET	If they do see thee, they will murder thee. 70
ROMEO	Alack there lies more peril in thine eye
	Than twenty of their swords; look thou but sweet,
	And I am proof against their enmity.
JULIET	I would not for the world they saw thee here.
ROMEO	I have night's cloak to hide me from their eyes,
	And but thou love me, let them find me here.
	My life were better ended by their hate,
	Than death prorogued, wanting of thy love.
JULIET	By whose direction found'st thou out this place?
ROMEO	By love that first did prompt me to inquire; 80
	He lent me counsel, and I lent him eyes.
	I am no pilot, yet wert thou as far
	As that vast shore washed with the farthest sea,
	I should adventure for such merchandise.
JULIET	Thou knowest the mask of night is on my face,
	Else would a maiden blush bepaint my cheek,
	For that which thou hast heard me speak tonight.
	Fain would I dwell on form, fain, fain deny
	What I have spoke; but farewell compliment.
	Dost thou love me? I know thou wilt say 'Ay', 90
	And I will take thy word. Yet if thou swearest,
	Thou mayst prove false; at lovers' perjuries

Juliet asks if he loves her, as she loves him. She wants
a simple answer, not one full of oaths. She is worried
that Romeo will think she is too 'forward'. Then she
says she must go.

Jove: king of the gods (Roman mythology)
perverse: difficult
but else ... world: But otherwise, I wouldn't behave in
    such a way for anything in the world
fond: foolishly (head over heels) in love
haviour light: behaviour 'forward'
those that have ... strange: girls who have more skill to
    play hard to get
But that: if it were not for the fact that
not impute ... love: do not put my willingness to love you
    down to frivolous love
discovered: revealed
That monthly ... orb: that changes her orbit every month
god of my idolatry: the god that I worship (idolize)
contract: exchange of statements of love
unadvised: ill thought out

They say Jove laughs. O gentle Romeo,
If thou dost love, pronounce it faithfully.
Or if thou thinkest I am too quickly won,
I'll frown and be perverse, and say thee nay,
So thou wilt woo; but else not for the world.
In truth fair Montague I am too fond,
And therefore thou mayst think my haviour light.
But trust me gentleman, I'll prove more true   100
Than those that have more cunning to be strange.
I should have been more strange, I must confess,
But that thou overheard'st, ere I was ware,
My true-love passion. Therefore pardon me,
And not impute this yielding to light love,
Which the dark night hath so dicovered.

ROMEO   Lady, by yonder blessed moon I vow,
That tips with silver all these fruit-tree tops–

JULIET   O swear not by the moon, th' inconstant moon,
That monthly changes in her circled orb,   110
Lest that thy love prove likewise variable.

ROMEO   What shall I swear by?

JULIET   Do not swear at all;
Or if thou wilt, swear by thy gracious self,
Which is the god of my idolatry,
And I'll believe thee.

ROMEO   If my heart's dear love–

JULIET   Well do not swear. Although I joy in thee,
I have no joy of this contract tonight.
It is too rash, too unadvised, too sudden;
Too like the lightning, which doth cease to be
Ere one can say, 'It lightens'. Sweet, good night.   120
This bud of love by summer's ripening breath
May prove a beauteous flower when next we meet.
Good night, good night. As sweet response and rest
Come to thy heart, as that within my breast.

ROMEO   O wilt thou leave me so unsatisfied?

JULIET   What satisfaction canst thou have tonight?

Romeo begs her at least to exchange vows of love with him. The Nurse calls Juliet away. When Juliet returns she says that she will send a messenger to Romeo that day to arrange a time and place where they can be married. Then she goes into the house.

I would: I wish
frank: generous
bounty: generosity
bent of love: intentions
procure: arrange
rite: ceremony

ROMEO	Th' exchange of thy love's faithful vow for mine.
JULIET	I gave thee mine before thou didst request it;
	And yet I would it were to give again.
ROMEO	Wouldst thou withdraw it? For what purpose, love?
JULIET	But to be frank and give it thee again. 131
	And yet I wish but for the thing I have.
	My bounty is as boundless as the sea,
	My love as deep; the more I give to thee
	The more I have, for both are infinite.
	I hear some noise within; dear love adieu.

[Nurse calls within

	Anon good Nurse! Sweet Montague, be true.
	Stay but a little, I will come again. *[Exit*
ROMEO	O blessed, blessed night! I am afeard,
	Being in night, all this is but a dream, 140
	Too flattering-sweet to be substantial.

Enter JULIET *again*

JULIET	Three words, dear Romeo, and good night indeed.
	If they thy bent of love be honourable,
	Thy purpose marriage, send me word tomorrow,
	By one that I'll procure to come to thee,
	Where and what time thou wilt perform the rite;
	And all my fortunes at thy foot I'll lay,
	And follow thee my lord throughout the world.
NURSE	[*Within*] Madam!
JULIET	I come, anon—But if thou meanest not well, 150
	I do beseech thee—
NURSE	[*Within*] Madam!
JULIET	By and by, I come—
	To cease thy strife, and leave me to my grief.
	Tomorrow will I send.
ROMEO	So thrive my soul—
JULIET	A thousand times good night. *[Exit*
ROMEO	A thousand times the worse, to want thy light.

A moment later Juliet returns; she has forgotten to fix a time at which Romeo will meet her messenger.

Love goes ... heavy looks: in other words two lovers go towards each other as fast as the schoolboy goes away from school, and vice-versa

tassel-gentle: male falcon. (They were highly prized by falconers. If one went off on its own, the falconer had to use a special call to bring it back again.)

Bondage ... aloud: Juliet is 'tied up' (in bondage) because she is not supposed to be speaking to a young man in this way so she has to use a loud whisper (hoarse) rather than calling him.

Echo: in mythology a nymph who was in love with Narcissus. She could not speak her love for him, but was condemned to repeat the end of whatever people said to her.

nyas: a young hawk that cannot yet fly

wanton: naughty child

gyves: chains

Love goes toward love as schoolboys from their
    books,
But love from love, toward school with heavy looks.

Enter JULIET *again*

JULIET	Hist, Romeo, hist! O for a falconer's voice,
	To lure this tassel-gentle back again.
	Bondage is hoarse, and may not speak aloud, 160
	Else would I tear the cave where Echo lies,
	And make her airy tongue more hoarse than mine
	With repetition of my 'Romeo'.
ROMEO	It is my soul that calls upon my name.
	How silver-sweet sound lovers' tongues by night,
	Like softest music to attending ears.
JULIET	Romeo!
ROMEO	My nyas?
JULIET	What o'clock tomorrow
	Shall I send to thee?
ROMEO	By the hour of nine.
JULIET	I will not fail; 'tis twenty year till then.
	I have forgot why I did call thee back. 170
ROMEO	Let me stand here till thou remember it.
JULIET	I shall forget, to have thee still stand there,
	Remembering how I love thy company.
ROMEO	And I'll still stay, to have thee still forget,
	Forgetting any other home but this.
JULIET	'Tis almost morning; I would have thee gone,
	And yet no farther than a wanton's bird,
	Who lets it hop a little from her hand,
	Like a poor prisoner in his twisted gyves,
	And with a silken thread plucks it back again, 180
	So loving-jealous of his liberty.
ROMEO	I would I were thy bird.
JULIET	Sweet, so would I.
	Yet I should kill thee with much cherishing.

At last they part: Juliet into the house and Romeo out of the garden and away.

crave: beg
my dear hap: the wonderful thing that has happened to me

Keeping track

Scene 1

1 Where is Romeo while Benvolio and Mercutio are speaking?
2 Can he hear them?
3 How do you know?

Scene 2

4 What does Romeo mean when he says, 'He jests at scars that never felt a wound'?
5 When is the first time in this scene that the lovers speak directly to each other?
6 What is each talking about at that point?
7 In lines 62-70 Juliet is concerned about two things. One is how Romeo got there. What is the other?
8 How does Romeo respond to her concerns?
9 What does Juliet say about the way she wants Romeo to speak of his love? (lines 90-111)
10 What arrangement do the two of them make at the end of the scene?

> Good night, good night. Parting is such sweet
>   sorrow,
> That I shall say 'Good night' till it be morrow.
>
> _[Exit_

ROMEO   Sleep dwell upon thine eyes, peace in thy breast.
Would I were sleep and peace, so sweet to rest.
Hence will I to my ghostly father's cell,
His help to crave, and my dear hap to tell.   _[Exit_

Discussion

1 Act 1 scene 5 and Act 2 scene 2 both contain very
important moments in the play: the first and second
meetings of the two lovers. In between comes Act 2 scene
1. What is the point of presenting this short scene:
   ● from a theatrical point of view?
   ● as far as the themes of the play are concerned?
2 Act 2 scene 1 begins with a number of soliloquies (see
Glossary, p288). 50 lines go by before the two lovers
speak directly to each other. What effect do you think
this has on the audience?
3 Romeo and Juliet both talk about love. Are there
important differences in the ways they speak about it?

Staging

Look at the illustrations of an Elizabethan theatre on
pages 6 and 7. Think about how Act 2 scenes 1 and 2
might be staged. Remember these points:
● There was no artificial lighting; the plays were
performed in daylight.
● There was no curtain with which to hide the stage
between scenes.

Describe how each scene might be performed: where the
actors would enter from; where they would stand and
move; where they would exit.

Drama

O Romeo, Romeo, wherefore art thou Romeo?
Groups of three or four.
This famous scene may seem sentimental and long winded
in today's world. However it is still possible that two young
people could find themselves in the situation of being in love
with someone from an enemy family... for example – a
Catholic boy and a Protestant girl in Belfast.

- Imagine you are teams of scriptwriters working on a
  modern production of Romeo and Juliet. Instead of the
  original 189 lines you have to rewrite it in only 14 lines.
- You can use some of the original words, but try to
  change it into the language you would use in this
  situation.
- Here is a breakdown of the scene to help you.
  1 - 32: Romeo describing Juliet's beauty (one line).
  38-49: Juliet wishing Romeo was not a Montague
  (one line).
  52-60: Juliet realises Romeo is there and Romeo says
  he will give up his name (two lines).
  62-78: Juliet worries about Romeo being seen. He is
  not (two lines).
  95-167: they exchange vows of love (four lines).
  167-168: they agree to meet the next day (two lines).
  169-189: they say goodbye (two lines)
- Try to capture the serious and passionate nature of
  the original.
1 Each group works on its section until a 14 line script is
  assembled.
2 The whole class discusses the final draft at a 'script
  conference'.
3 Two actors speak the new lines.

4 The rest of the class helps with advice. Remember to think about the non-verbal messages.

Character

1 Juliet
You have now seen Juliet in two scenes. Think about your first impressions of her. Is she just a female version of Romeo, or do you get a distinct and different picture of her character in these scenes?
2 Add to your Character logs for:
Benvolio, Mercutio, Romeo, Juliet

Close study

Lines 85-136

1 Look carefully at Juliet's first speech. What is Juliet saying in lines 90-4?
2 What is she concerned about in the rest of the speech? Why is this?
3 What do you think Romeo was going to say in lines 107-8? Why does Juliet interrupt him?
4 Why does Juliet try to end the conversation in lines 123-4?
5 Shakespeare could rely on no artificial stage effects or scenery. In this section how does he convey to the audience the time and place of the conversation?

Quiz

Light and dark

Find the exact words in which:
1 Romeo describes the dawn coming.
2 Benvolio says that the dark is the best place for Romeo's love.
3 Juliet says that the night is almost over.
4 Romeo compares Juliet to the sun.
5 Juliet tells Romeo not to swear by the moon.

Comparisons

Who compares whom or what to:

6 a male falcon

7 an attendant on the moon goddess.

Romeo visits his confessor and spiritual adviser, Friar Lawrence. He finds the Friar collecting herbs.

1 Friar Lawrence is up early, collecting poisonous and healing herbs in a wicker basket.

2 He observes that the earth is both a tomb, where all life goes when it dies, and a womb from which all new life comes.

3 The earth produces a great variety of plants and they are all useful in different ways.

4 There is nothing living that doesn't have some special value and nothing is so good that cannot go wrong if abused.

8 a flower bud
9 the sea
10 a pet bird on a string.

Outside Friar Lawrence's cell
Enter FRIAR LAWRENCE *with a basket*

F. LAWRENCE The gray-eyed morn smiles on the frowning night,
Chequering the eastern clouds with streaks of light;
And fleckled darkness like a drunkard reels
From forth day's path and Titan's burning wheels.
Now ere the sun advance his burning eye,
The day to cheer, and night's dank dew to dry,
I must up-fill this osier cage of ours
With baleful weeds, and precious-juiced flowers.
The earth that's nature's mother is her tomb;
What is her burying grave, that is her womb;   10
And from her womb children of divers kind
We sucking on her natural bosom find;
Many for many virtues excellent,
None but for some, and yet all different.
O mickle is the powerful grace that lies
In plants, herbs, stones, and their true qualities.
For nought so vile that on the earth doth live,
But to the earth some special good doth give,
Nor aught so good, but strained from that fair use,
Revolts from true birth, stumbling on abuse.   20
Virtue itself turns vice being misapplied,
And vice sometime's by action dignified.

Enter ROMEO

It is very early in the morning and Friar Lawrence deduces correctly that Romeo has been out all night. Romeo admits this.

5

6

5 For example, he says, the skin of this plant contains both poison and medicine: if you smell it, it does you good; if you swallow it, you die.

6 People are the same; they contain both good and evil in their make up.

Benedicite: (Latin) God bless you

it argues ... bed: being up so early suggests that you are worried about something

Care keeps ... lie: old men have plenty to worry about and if you are worried you don't sleep well

unstuffed: unworried

up-roused by some distemperature: awoken by some worry

ghostly: spiritual

one hath wounded ... wounded: someone wounded me (with love) and I wounded them in the same way

physic: medicine

My intercession ... foe: The request I am making to you will also help my 'enemy'

thy drift: what you are saying

Riddling confession ... shrift: If you confess to me using words I can't understand, you will only get a forgiveness that you can't understand.

Within the infant rind of this weak flower
Poison hath residence, and medicine power;
For this being smelt with that part cheers each part;
Being tasted, stays all senses with the heart.
Two such opposed kings encamp them still
In man as well as herbs–grace and rude will;
And where the worser is predominant,
Full soon the canker death eats up that plant.   30

ROMEO   Good morrow father.

F. LAWRENCE   *Benedicite!*
What early tongue so sweet saluteth me?
Young son, it argues a distempered head
So soon to bid good morrow to thy bed.
Care keeps his watch in every old man's eye,
And where care lodges, sleep will never lie;
But where unbruised youth with unstuffed brain
Doth couch his limbs, there golden sleep doth reign.
Therefore thy earliness doth me assure
Thou art up-roused by some distemperature;   40
Or if not so, then here I hit it right,
Our Romeo hath not been in bed tonight.

ROMEO   That last is true; the sweeter rest was mine.

F. LAWRENCE   God pardon sin, wast thou with Rosaline?

ROMEO   With Rosaline, my ghostly father? No.
I have forgot that name, and that name's woe.

F. LAWRENCE   That's my good son; but where hast thou been
then?

ROMEO   I'll tell thee ere thou ask it me again.
I have been feasting with mine enemy,
Where on a sudden one hath wounded me,   50
That's by me wounded; both our remedies
Within thy help and holy physic lies.
I bear no hatred, blessed man; for lo,
My intercession likewise steads my foe.

F. LAWRENCE   Be plain good son, and homely in thy drift;
Riddling confession finds but riddling shrift.

Romeo tells Friar Lawrence that he has fallen in love with Juliet, a Capulet. Friar Lawrence points out that only yesterday he was just as deeply in love with Rosaline. He points out that Romeo's love for Rosaline was not true love.

pass: go along

brine: salt water

sallow: pale

If e'er ... Rosaline: If you were being yourself and talking about real unhappiness, then both you and your unhappiness were all about Rosaline

sentence: proverb

Women may fall ... men: When men are weak then what hope is there for women?

chidst me: told me off

doting ... loving: for being infatuated (imagining you were in love) not for truly loving

badst me: told me to

her I love ... allow: The person I love now gives me favours in return for the favours I give her; she shares her love with me as I share mine with her.

Thy love ... spell: Your love was like someone who 'reads' by learning the story by heart but cannot spell out the letters of what is written.

ROMEO   Then plainly know my heart's dear love is set
             On the fair daughter of rich Capulet.
             As mine on hers, so hers is set on mine,
             And all combined, save what thou must combine 60
             By holy marriage. When, and where, and how,
             We met, we wooed, and made exchange of vow,
             I'll tell thee as we pass; but this I pray,
             That thou consent to marry us today.

F. LAWRENCE Holy Saint Francis, what a change is here!
             Is Rosaline, whom thou didst love so dear,
             So soon forsaken? Young men's love then lies
             Not truly in their hearts, but in their eyes.
             Jesu Maria, what a deal of brine
             Hath washed thy sallow cheeks for Rosaline!   70
             How much salt water thrown away in waste,
             To season love, that of it doth not taste!
             The sun not yet thy sighs from heaven clears,
             Thy old groans yet ring in mine ancient ears;
             Lo here upon thy cheek the stain doth sit
             Of an old tear that is not washed off yet.
             If e'er thou wast thyself, and these woes thine,
             Thou and these woes were all for Rosaline.
             And art thou changed? Pronounce this sentence
                then,
             Women may fall, when there's no strength in
                men.   80

ROMEO   Thou chid'st me oft for loving Rosaline.

F. LAWRENCE For doting, not for loving, pupil mine.

ROMEO   And bad'st me bury love.

F. LAWRENCE   Not in a grave,
             To lay one in another out to have.

ROMEO   I pray thee chide me not; her I love now
             Doth grace for grace, and love for love allow.
             The other did not so.

F.LAWRENCE   O she knew well
             Thy love did read by rote, that could not spell.

Friar Lawrence accepts that Romeo's love for Juliet may be true love and that the relationship between them may serve to bring their warring families together.

Later that morning Mercutio and Benvolio are still looking for Romeo. Tybalt has sent a letter (probably a challenge) to Romeo's home.

waverer: person who keeps on changing his/her mind
alliance: marriage (but also an alliance between the two families)
rancour: hatred

1 Mercutio and Benvolio are still looking for Romeo; they know he hasn't been home. Mercutio blames Rosaline.
2 Benvolio tells him that Tybalt has sent a letter to Romeo. Mercutio suggests it is a challenge to fight a duel. If so, says Benvolio, Romeo will answer it.
3 Mercutio complains that love has already killed the real Romeo and he is in no state to face Tybalt.

> But come young waverer, come go with me.
> In one respect I'll thy assistant be;   90
> For this alliance may so happy prove,
> To turn your households' rancour to pure love.

ROMEO   O let us hence, I stand on sudden haste.

F. LAWRENCE Wisely and slow, they stumble that run fast.

> *[Exeunt*

SCENE 4

A street in Verona
Enter BENVOLIO *and* MERCUTIO

MERCUTIO   Where the devil should this Romeo be?
            Came he not home tonight?

BENVOLIO   Not to his father's; I spoke with this man.

MERCUTIO   Why, that same pale hard-hearted wench, that
               Rosaline,
            Torments him so, that he will sure run mad.

BENVOLIO   Tybalt, the kinsman to old Capulet,
            Hath sent a letter to his father's house.

MERCUTIO   A challenge, on my life.

BENVOLIO   Romeo will answer it.

MERCUTIO   Any man that can write may answer a letter.

BENVOLIO   Nay, he will answer the letter's master, how he 10
            dares, being dared.

MERCUTIO   Alas poor Romeo, he is already dead, stabbed with
            a white wench's black eye, run through the
            ear with a lovesong, the very pin of his heart cleft
            with the blind bow-boy's butt-shaft; and is he a
            man to encounter Tybalt?

BENVOLIO   Why what is Tybalt?

MERCUTIO   More than Prince of Cats. O he is the

Mercutio comments that Tybalt loves duelling and knows all the latest fencing styles. Romeo arrives and greets them.

4 Tybalt is an expert swordsman who knows all the latest fencing techniques.
5 Mercutio pours scorn on all these fashionable young men with their affected behaviour.
6 Romeo arrives and Mercutio makes fun of him and his love.
7 Romeo asks what is troubling them and excuses his disappearance the night before.

courageous captain of compliments. He fights as you sing prick-song, keeps time, distance, and proportion; rests his minim rests, one, two, and the third in your bosom; the very butcher of a silk button, a duellist, a duellist; a gentleman of the very first house, of the first and second cause. Ah the immortal *passado*, the *punto reverso*, the hay!   26

BENVOLIO   The what?

MERCUTIO   The pox of such antic lisping affecting phantacimes, these new tuners of accents! 'By Jesu a very good blade–a very tall man–a very good whore!' Why, is not this a lamentable thing, grandsire, that we should be thus afflicted with these strange flies, these fashion-mongers, these 'pardon-me's', who stand so much on the new form that they cannot sit at ease on the old bench? O their bones, their bones!   36

Enter ROMEO

BENVOLIO   Here comes Romeo, here comes Romeo.

MERCUTIO   Without his roe, like a dried herring. O flesh, flesh, how art thou fishified! Now is he for the numbers that Petrarch flowed in. Laura to his lady was a kitchen-wench–marry, she had a better love to be-rhyme her–Dido a dowdy, Cleopatra a gipsy, Helen and Hero hildings and harlots, Thisbe a gray eye or so, but not to the purpose–Signior Romeo, *bon jour*. There's a French salutation to your French slop. You gave us the counterfeit fairly last night.

ROMEO   Good morrow to you both. What counterfeit did I give you?

MERCUTIO   The slip sir, the slip, can you not conceive?   50

ROMEO   Pardon good Mercutio, my business was great, and in such a case as mine a man may strain

Romeo is in fine form and is more than a match for Mercutio's skill with words.

8 Romeo and Mercutio then engage in a battle of words, using many puns and other fanciful expressions. Romeo shows that in his present mood he is more than a match for Mercutio.

	courtesy.
MERCUTIO	That's as much as to say, such a case as yours constrains a man to bow in the hams.
ROMEO	Meaning to curtsy.
MERCUTIO	Thou hast most kindly hit it.
ROMEO	A most courteous exposition.
MERCUTIO	Nay I am the very pink of courtesy.
ROMEO	Pink for flower.
MERCUTIO	Right.
ROMEO	Why then is my pump well flowered.
MERCUTIO	Sure wit. Follow me this jest now, till thou hast worn out thy pump, that when the single sole of it is worn, the jest may remain after the wearing solely singular.
ROMEO	O single-soled jest, solely singular for the singleness.
MERCUTIO	Come between us good Benvolio, my wits faint.
ROMEO	Switch and spurs, switch and spurs, or I'll cry a match.
MERCUTIO	Nay, if our wits run the wild-goose chase, I am done; for thou hast more of the wild-goose in one of thy wits than I am sure I have in my whole five. Was I with you there for the goose?
ROMEO	Thou wast never with me for anything when thou wast not there for the goose.
MERCUTIO	I will bite thee by the ear for that jest.
ROMEO	Nay good goose, bite not.
MERCUTIO	Thy wit is a very bitter sweeting, it is a most sharp sauce.
ROMEO	And is it not then well served in to a sweet goose?
MERCUTIO	O here's a wit of cheverel that stretches from an inch narrow to an ell broad.
ROMEO	I stretch it out for that word 'broad', which,

60

71

80

**When the Nurse and her attendant Peter come
looking for Romeo, the three young men tease her
mercilessly.**

9

9 Mercutio tells him that this is more like the old
   Romeo they all know.

God ye: God give you
the bawdy … noon: Mercutio tells her the time in a
   deliberately obscene way
mar: spoil

	added to the goose proves thee far and wide a broad goose.
MERCUTIO	Why, is not this better now than groaning for love? Now art thou sociable, now art thou Romeo. Now art thou what thou art, by art as well as by nature, for this drivelling love is like a great natural that runs lolling up and down to hide his bauble in a hole.
BENVOLIO	Stop there, stop there.
MERCUTIO	Thou desirest me to stop in my tale against the hair.
BENVOLIO	Thou wouldst else have made thy tale large.
MERCUTIO	O thou art deceived; I would have made it short, for I was come to the whole depth of my tale, and meant indeed to occupy the argument no longer.

Enter NURSE *and* PETER

ROMEO	Here's goodly gear! A sail, a sail!
MERCUTIO	Two, two; a shirt and a smock.
NURSE	Peter.
PETER	Anon.
NURSE	My fan Peter.
MERCUTIO	Good Peter, to hide her face, for her fan's the fairer face.
NURSE	God ye good morrow gentlemen.
MERCUTIO	God ye good den fair gentlewomen.
NURSE	Is it good den?
MERCUTIO	'Tis no less, I tell ye, for the bawdy hand of the dial is now upon the prick of noon.
NURSE	Out upon you, what a man are you!
ROMEO	One, gentlewoman, that God hath made for himself to mar.
NURSE	By my troth, it is well said 'for himself to mar', quoth a! Gentlemen, can any of you tell me

94

100

110

At last Mercutio and Benvolio leave and the Nurse can speak to Romeo.

confidence: private conversation
indite: invite
a bawd: a person who keeps a brothel (Mercutio is
  suggesting that the Nurse wants to make an improper
  suggestion to Romeo)
So ho!: a hunting call used when the game has been
  sighted
lenten pie: during Lent no meat was eaten, so a hare pie
  would be stale, having been made before Lent
hoar: grey with age (but a play on words with whore
  (prostitute) and hare)
spent: used up
ropery: trickery
stand to: put up with
'a: he
lustier: stronger
Jacks: villains
scurvy knave: wicked villain
flirt-gills: women of loose morals

	where I may find the young Romeo?
ROMEO	I can tell you, but young Romeo will be older 120 when you have found him, than he was when you sought him. I am the youngest of that name, for fault of a worse.
NURSE	You say well.
MERCUTIO	Yea, is the worst well? Very well took, i' faith, wisely, wisely.
NURSE	If you be he sir, I desire some confidence with you.
BENVOLIO	She will indite him to some supper.
MERCUTIO	A bawd, a bawd, a bawd! So ho!
ROMEO	What hast thou found? 130
MERCUTIO	No hare sir, unless a hare sir in a lenten pie, that is something stale and hoar ere it be spent. [*Sings*

An old hare hoar,
And an old hare hoar,
Is very good meat in Lent.
But a hare that is hoar
Is too much for a score,
When it hoars ere it be spent.

MERCUTIO	Romeo, will you come to your father's? We'll to dinner thither. 140
ROMEO	I will follow you.
MERCUTIO	Farewell ancient lady, farewell, [*Sings* lady, lady, lady. [*Exeunt Mercutio and Benvolio*
NURSE	I pray you sir, what saucy merchant was this that was so full of his ropery?
ROMEO	A gentleman, Nurse, that loves to hear himself talk, and will speak more in a minute than he will stand to in a month.
NURSE	And 'a speak any thing against me, I'll take him down, an 'a were lustier than he is, and twenty such Jacks; and if I cannot, I'll find those that shall. Scurvy knave, I am none of his flirt-gills, I

The Nurse gives Romeo her message, but not before expressing her indignation at the way she has been treated and giving Romeo a warning about treating Juliet properly. Then she arranges with Romeo that Juliet will go to Friar Lawrence's cell that afternoon to be married.

skain's-mates: women of loose morals

suffer: allow

use me at his pleasure: take advantage of me. (She means 'make fun' of her, but it has an accidental bawdy double meaning, which she doesn't realise)

I saw ... been out: Peter repeats the double meaning (not realising it) and his comment about his 'weapon' only makes it worse

bade me inquire you out: told me to find you by asking around

lead her in a fool's paradise: seduce her by pretending to offer marriage

gross: wicked

deal double with: cheat

commend me to: give my greetings to

dost not mark: are not listening to

shrift: confession

shrived and married: before marriage the couple confessed their sins and were given absolution (forgiveness)

	am none of his skain's-mates. [*To Peter*] And thou must stand by too, and suffer every knave to use me at his pleasure?
PETER	I saw no man use you at his pleasure. If I had, my weapon should quickly have been out, I warrant you; I dare draw as soon as another man, if I see occasion in a good quarrel, and the law on my side. 160
NURSE	Now afore God I am so vexed, that every part about me quivers. Scurvy knave! Pray you sir a word and as I told you, my young lady bade me inquire you out. What she bade me say, I will keep to myself. But first let me tell ye, if ye should lead her in a fool's paradise, as they say, it were a very gross kind of behaviour, as they say; for the gentlewoman is young, and therefore if you should deal double with her, truly it were an ill thing to be offered to any gentlewoman, and very weak dealing. 171
ROMEO	Nurse, commend me to thy lady and mistress. I, protest unto thee–
NURSE	Good heart, and i' faith, I will tell her as much. Lord, Lord, she will be a joyful woman.
ROMEO	What wilt thou tell her, Nurse? thou dost not mark me
NURSE	I will tell her sir, that you do protest, which as I take it is a gentlemanlike offer.
ROMEO	Bid her devise 180 Some means to come to shrift this afternoon, And there she shall at Friar Lawrence' cell Be shrived and married. Here is for thy pains.
NURSE	No truly sir, not a penny.
ROMEO	Go to, I say you shall.
NURSE	This afternoon sir? Well, she shall be there.
ROMEO	And stay good Nurse behind the abbey wall,

They also arrange that a rope ladder will be hidden at the Capulets' house for Romeo to get in that night.

cords ... stair: a rope ladder
which to the ... night: which must carry me under cover of darkness to the summit of my happiness
quit thy pains: pay you for your trouble
Two may ... away: two people can keep a secret, but three can't (a proverb)
warrant thee: I promise you
prating: chattering
would fain ... aboard: has designs on her
had as lief: would as soon
properer: better-looking
clout: rag, piece of cloth
the versal world: the whole world
rosemary: a herb that was said to stand for remembrance
that's the dog's name: (because if you say 'R' it sounds like a dog growling)
sententious: she means 'sentence' - ie a saying

Within this hour my man shall be with thee,
And bring thee cords made like a tackled stair,
Which to the high top-gallant of my joy   190
Must be my convoy in the secret night.
Farewell, be trusty, and I'll quit thy pains.
Farewell, commend me to thy mistress.

NURSE   Now God in heaven bless thee. Hark you sir.

ROMEO   What sayest thou my dear Nurse?

NURSE   Is your man secret? Did you ne'er hear say,
Two may keep counsel, putting one away?

ROMEO   I warrant thee my man's as true as steel.   198

NURSE   Well sir, my mistress is the sweetest lady. Lord,
Lord, when 't was a little prating thing. O there
is a nobleman in town, one Paris, that would fain
lay knife aboard; but she good soul had as lief see
a toad, a very toad, as see him. I anger her
sometimes, and tell her that Paris is the properer
man; but I'll warrant you when I say so, she
looks as pale as any clout in the versal world.
Doth not rosemary and Romeo begin both with
a letter?

ROMEO   Ay Nurse, what of that? Both with an R?   209

NURSE   Ah mocker, that's the dog-name; R is for the–no,
I know it begins with some other letter. And she
hath the prettiest sententious of it, of you
and rosemary, that it would do you good to hear
it.

ROMEO   Commend me to thy lady.

NURSE   Ay, a thousand times. Peter!

PETER   Anon.

NURSE   Before and apace.   [*Exeunt*

ACTIVITIES

Keeping track

Scene 3

1 Why is Friar Lawrence surprised to see Romeo?
2 When Romeo explains, why does Friar Lawrence find this surprising?
3 What does he think about Romeo's love for Rosaline?
4 What does he think about Romeo's love for Juliet?

Scene 4

5 With which earlier scene is this one linked?
6 What have Benvolio and Mercutio been doing in the meantime?
7 How does Mercutio find Romeo has changed since they last met, and what is his response?
8 How do the three young men treat the Nurse and how does she respond?
9 What arrangements do the Nurse and Romeo make?

Discussion

Attitudes to love

Act 2 scenes 1-4 offer different attitudes to love:
- Mercutio's (2/1, 2/4 lines 1-47)
- Friar Lawrence's (2/3)
- Romeo's (2/2)
- Juliet's (2/2)

How would you describe each of these?

Drama

'a gentleman that loves to hear himself talk'

In pairs.

Mercutio has a way with words and has great fun sparring with his friends - each trying to better the other with a turn of phrase or clever riposte. The best way to appreciate this is to say the words out loud and, if you can, learn them.

1 Practise one of the following short speeches, from scene 4
   ● 12 - 16 Alas poor Romeo ...
   ● 18 - 26 More than a Prince of Cats.
   ● 28 - 36 The pox of such antic ...
   ● 38 - 47 Without his roe ...
2 Try to understand as much as you can of what he says, but remember that he enjoys the sounds as much as the meaning of words.
3 Learn them and enjoy them, they are meant to be fun.

Follow-up.

Romeo is an equal sparring partner - the two of them probably enjoy fencing with words as much as with rapiers - and it is less painful! In pairs practise and learn the exchanges between them in lines 48 - 98.

Character

Character logs

Start a Character log for Friar Lawrence. Add to your Character logs for Benvolio, Mercutio, Romeo and Nurse.

Mercutio

The end of Act 2 scene 4 provides a good moment to reflect on the character of Mercutio. Look at your Character log and then think about these questions:

1 What would each of these characters say about Mercutio's behaviour?

Nurse, Benvolio, Romeo
2 What can you say about each of these aspects of
  Mercutio's character?
  ● his command of language
  ● his imagination
  ● his attitude towards fashion
  ● his attitude towards love and sex

Writing

What do you think Romeo does immediately after this
scene? Does he:
● go home and meet his parents
● find Benvolio and Mercutio and talk to them again
● go off on his own and think his own thoughts
● do something else?

Think about this and then write about what Romeo does
next. Write it as:
● a story with direct speech (and 'thoughts'), or
● a script, or
● a poem.

Juliet waits impatiently for the Nurse to return.

Perchance: perhaps
lowering: overhanging, threatening
nimble-pinioned: swift-winged
draw love: in classical pictures doves were shown drawing
  a chariot containing Venus the goddess of love

Quiz

1 Who *knew well* whose *love did read by rote and could not spell?*
2 Who is a *gentleman ... that loves to hear himself talk?*
3 Whose *love then lies/Not truly in their hearts but in their eyes?*
4 Who refuses a tip?
5 Who is *that same pale hard-hearted wench?*
6 Without looking back at the text, try to complete the blanks in this quotation. (Clue: the lines rhyme)
   If e'er thou wast thyself, and these woes ____,
   Thou and these ____ were all for Rosaline.
   And art ____ changed? Pronounce this sentence then:
   Women may fall when there's no strength in ____.

SCENE 5

Capulet's mansion
Enter JULIET

JULIET   The clock struck nine when I did send the Nurse;
          In half an hour she promised to return.
          Perchance she cannot meet him–that's not so–
          O she is lame, love's heralds should be thoughts,
          Which ten times faster glides than the sun's beams,
          Driving back shadows over lowering hills.
          Therefore do nimble-pinioned doves draw love,
          And therefore hath the wind-swift Cupid wings
          Now is the sun upon the highmost hill
          Of this day's journey, and from nine to twelve   10
          Is three long hours, yet she is not come.
          Had she affections and warm youthful blood,

When the Nurse returns, she is in no hurry to tell Juliet what has happened. She teases Juliet by delaying her news as long as possible.

bandy: send back (as in tennis)
feign as: act as if
give me leave: leave me alone
jaunt: tiring journey
stay the circumstance: wait for the details of your message
flower: model

She would be swift in motion as a ball;
My words would bandy her to my sweet love,
And his to me.
But old folks, many feign as they were dead,
Unwieldy, slow, heavy and pale as lead.
O God she comes! O honey Nurse what news?

Enter NURSE *and* PETER

Hast thou met with him? Send thy man away. 19
NURSE   Peter, stay at the gate.   [*Exit Peter*
JULIET   Now good sweet Nurse–O Lord why lookest
              thou sad?
           Though news be sad, yet tell them merrily.
           If good, thou sham'st the music of sweet news
           By playing it to me with so sour a face.
NURSE   I am aweary, give me leave awhile.
           Fie how my bones ache, what a jaunt have I?
JULIET   I would thou hadst my bones, and I thy news.
           Nay come I pray thee speak, good, good, Nurse
              speak.
NURSE   Jesu, what haste! Can you not stay awhile?
           Do you not see that I am out of breath?   30
JULIET   How art thou out of breath, when thou hast breath
           To say to me that thou art out of breath?
           The excuse that thou dost make in this delay
           Is longer than the tale thou dost excuse.
           Is thy news good or bad? Answer to that.
           Say either, and I'll stay the circumstance.
           Let me be satisfied, is't good or bad?
NURSE   Well, you have made a simple choice, you know
           not how to choose a man. Romeo? No, not he.
           Though his face be better than any man's, yet 40
           his leg excels all men's; and for a hand, and a
           foot, and a body, though they be not to be talked
           on, yet they are past compare. He is not the
           flower of courtesy, but I'll warrant him, as gentle

Eventually the Nurse tells Juliet the arrangement: that she is to go to Friar Lawrence's cell to meet Romeo and be married to him.

Beshrew: curse
jauncing: travelling busily
within: indoors
hot: impatient
poultice: dressing
coil: to-do
drudge: lowly servant

as a lamb. Go thy ways wench, serve God. What,
have you dined at home?

JULIET No, no. But all this did I know before.
What says he of our marriage, what of that?

NURSE Lord, how my head aches, what a head have I!
It beats as it would fall in twenty pieces.   50
My back a t' other side, ah my back, my back!
Beshrew your heart for sending me about,
To catch my death with jauncing up and down.

JULIET I' faith I am sorry that thou art not well.
Sweet, sweet, sweet nurse, tell me what says my
    love?

NURSE Your love says, like an honest gentleman, and a
courteous, and a kind, and a handsome, and I
warrant a virtuous–Where is your mother?

JULIET Where is my mother? Why she is within.
Where should she be? How oddly thou repliest.
'Your love says like an honest gentleman,
"Where is your mother?"'

NURSE   O God's lady dear,   62
Are you so hot? Marry come up I trow,
Is this the poultice for my aching bones?
Henceforward do your messages yourself.

JULIET Here's such a coil. Come, what says Romeo?

NURSE Have you got leave to go to shrift today?

JULIET I have.

NURSE Then hie you hence to Friar Lawrence' cell,
There stays a husband to make you a wife.   70
Now comes the wanton blood up in your cheeks,
They'll be in scarlet straight at any news.
Hie you to church. I must another way,
To fetch a ladder by the which your love
Must climb a bird's nest soon when it is dark.
I am the drudge, and toil in your delight.
But you shall bear the burden soon at night.

Romeo and Friar Lawrence await Juliet's arrival. Romeo is impatient and the Friar tries to persuade him to be patient. Juliet arrives.

So smile ... not!: May heaven bless this ceremony so that afterwards there is no cause for unhappiness.
come what sorrow can: whatever sorrow may come
countervail: equal
These violent ... ends: Extreme emotions such as your love for Juliet often end violently
in their triumph: at the moment of their greatest success
powder: gunpowder
tardy: late
Is loathsome ... deliciousness: can become sickly just because it is so sweet
confounds: destroys
bestride the ... summer air: walk on the strands of spiders' web floating in the light summer breeze
ghostly: spiritual

Go. I'll to dinner. Hie you to the cell!

JULIET   Hie to high fortune! Honest Nurse farewell.

                                      [*Exeunt*

SCENE 6

Friar Lawrence's cell
Enter FRIAR LAWRENCE *and* ROMEO

F. LAWRENCE   So smile the heavens upon this holy act,
              That after hours with sorrow chide us not.

ROMEO   Amen, amen, but come what sorrow can,
              It cannot countervail the exchange of joy
              That one short minute gives me in her sight.
              Do thou but close our hands with holy words,
              Then love-devouring death do what he dare,
              It is enough I may but call her mine.

F. LAWRENCE   These violent delights have violent ends,
              And in their triumph die, like fire and powder,   10
              Which as they kiss consume. The sweetest honey
              Is loathsome in his own deliciousness,
              And in the taste confounds the appetite.
              Therefore love moderately, long love doth so;
              Too swift arrives as tardy as too slow.

              Enter JULIET *somewhat fast, and embraceth* ROMEO

              Here comes the lady. O so light a foot
              Will ne'er wear out the everlasting flint.
              A lover may bestride the gossamers
              That idles in the wanton summer air,
              And yet not fall; so light is vanity.   20

JULIET   Good even to my ghostly confessor.

F. LAWRENCE Romeo shall thank thee daughter for us both.

JULIET   As much to him, else is his thanks too much.

Juliet and Romeo exchange declarations of love. Then the Friar leads them off to be married.

measure ... be heaped: The idea is of a jug used to measure dry goods like flour. If it is heaped up, you get more than the full measure.

blazon: make public

that both ... encounter: that we each get from each other in this meeting

Conceit, more rich ... wealth: Juliet does not like Romeo's extravagant style of speech. She tells him: 'True imagination is wealthier in real things than in words and so can talk about reality and not mere decoration. People who can actually count up their wealth are only poor. My own true love has grown so great that I cannot even count up half my wealth.'

ROMEO   Ah, Juliet, if the measure of thy joy
          Be heaped like mine, and that thy skill be more
          To blazon it, then sweeten with thy breath
          This neighbour air, and let rich music's tongue
          Unfold the imagined happiness that both
          Receive in either by this dear encounter.
JULIET   Conceit, more rich in matter than in words   30
          Brags of his substance, not of ornament.
          They are but beggars that can count their worth.
          But my true love is grown to such excess,
          I cannot sum up sum of half my wealth.
F. LAWRENCE Come, come with me, and we will make short
               work.
          For by your leaves, you shall not stay alone,
          Till holy church incorporate two in one.
                                              [*Exeunt*

In the heat of the day Benvolio and Mercutio are in the street. Benvolio wants Mercutio to withdraw because the Capulets are about and looking for trouble. Mercutio refuses: if anything, he says, Benvolio is the troublemaker.

1 Benvolio begs Mercutio to go indoors since the Capulets are around and in this hot weather there could well be trouble.

2 Mercutio retorts that Benvolio is a fine one to talk: he is as much a troublemaker as anyone.

3 Mercutio lists a number of crazy reasons (all, presumably, made up) that Benvolio has had for picking quarrels with people.

Act three

Verona. A public place.
Enter MERCUTIO, BENVOLIO, *and men*

BENVOLIO   I pray thee good Mercutio, let's retire.
The day is hot, the Capels are abroad,
And if we meet, we shall not 'scape a brawl,
For now these hot days, is the mad blood stirring.

MERCUTIO   Thou art like one of these fellows that when he
enters the confines of a tavern, claps me his
sword upon the table, and says, 'God send me
no need of thee;' and by the operation of the
second cup, draws him on the drawer, when
indeed there is no need.   10

BENVOLIO   Am I like such a fellow?

MERCUTIO   Come, come, thou art as hot a Jack in thy mood
as any in Italy, and as soon moved to be moody,
and as soon moody to be moved.

BENVOLIO   And what to?

MERCUTIO   Nay and there were two such, we should have
none shortly, for one would kill the other. Thou?
Why thou wilt quarrel with a man that hath a
hair more, or a hair less, in his beard than thou
hast. Thou wilt quarrel with a man for cracking
nuts, having no other reason but because thou
hast hazel eyes. What eye, but such an eye,
would spy out such a quarrel? Thy head is as full
of quarrels as an egg is full of meat, and yet thy
head hath been beaten as addle as an egg for
quarrelling. Thou hast quarrelled with a man for
coughing in the street, because he hath wakened
thy dog that hath lain asleep in the sun. Didst

Tybalt and his companions approach them, looking for Romeo. Mercutio looks for a fight, while Benvolio urges caution. Romeo arrives.

4   Benvolio is just defending himself against this charge when Tybalt and other Capulets approach them.

apt: ready

an: if

consortest: go around with

Consort?: Mercutio takes the word in its other sense, of a group of musicians

minstrels: travelling musicians

An thou ... discords: if you turn us into musicians, be prepared to hear nothing but discords.

my fiddlestick: my sword

'Zounds: an oath which comes from the expression 'God's wounds'.

public haunt of men: public place

I will not ... pleasure: I'm not going to move to please anyone.

my man: the person I am looking for (Mercutio deliberately misunderstands Tybalt and takes him to mean 'my servant'.)

livery: servant's uniform

thou not fall out with a tailor for wearing his new
doublet before Easter? With another for tying his
new shoes with old riband? And yet thou wilt
tutor me from quarrelling.   32

BENVOLIO   And I were so apt to quarrel as thou art, any
man should buy the fee-simple of my life for an
hour and a quarter.

MERCUTIO   The fee-simple? O simple!

Enter TYBALT, PETRUCHIO, *and others*

BENVOLIO   By my head, here comes the Capulets.

MERCUTIO   By my heel, I care not.

TYBALT   Follow me close, for I will speak to them.
Gentlemen, good den; a word with one of you.   40

MERCUTIO   And but one word with one of us? Couple it with
something, make it a word and a blow.

TYBALT   You shall find me apt enough to that sir, an you
will give me occasion.

MERCUTIO   Could you not take some occasion without giving?

TYBALT   Mercutio, thou consortest with Romeo.

MERCUTIO   Consort? What, dost thou make us minstrels? An
thou make minstrels of us, look to hear nothing
but discords. Here's my fiddlestick, here's that
shall make you dance. Zounds, consort!   50

BENVOLIO   We talk here in the public haunt of men.
Either withdraw into some private place,
And reason coldly of your grievances,
Or else depart; here all eyes gaze on us.

MERCUTIO   Men's eyes were made to look, and let them
         gaze.
I will not budge for no man's pleasure, I.

Enter ROMEO

TYBALT   Well, peace be with you sir, here comes my man.

MERCUTIO   But I'll be hanged sir, if he wear your livery.

**Tybalt insults Romeo in an attempt to provoke a
fight, but Romeo responds calmly and will not take up
the challenge. Mercutio is incensed at this apparent
cowardice and challenges Tybalt. They fight. Romeo
tries to stop the fight and in the confusion Tybalt
stabs Mercutio.**

Marry go ... man: You lead the way to the duelling field
and he will follow, that's the only sense in which you can
call him 'man'. (i.e. as a man of honour)

excuse the ... greeting: allow me to ignore the anger that
such a greeting would normally produce.

Boy: an insulting form of address

devise: imagine

tender: hold

Alla stoccata: a term from fencing

rat-catcher: Mercutio is referring to Tybalt's name, which
in the story of Reynard the Fox was that of the cat
(similar to the modern 'Tibby')

as you shall use me hereafter: depending on how you
treat me after this

dry-beat: beat with a stick

pilcher: scabbard

forbear: stop

bandying: quarrelling

Marry go before to field, he'll be your follower;
Your worship in that sense may call him man. 60

TYBALT   Romeo, the love I bear thee can afford
No better term than this-thou art a villain.

ROMEO   Tybalt, the reason that I have to love thee
Doth much excuse the appertaining rage
To such a greeting. Villain am I none.
Therefore farewell, I see thou knowest me not.

TYBALT   Boy, this shall not excuse the injuries
That thou hast done me, therefore turn and draw.

ROMEO   I do protest I never injured thee,
But love thee better than thou canst devise.   70
Till thou shalt know the reason of my love.
And so good Capulet, which name I tender
As dearly as my own, be satisfied.

MERCUTIO   O calm, dishonourable, vile submission!
Alla stoccata carries it away.
Tybalt, you rat-catcher, will you walk?

TYBALT   What wouldst thou have with me?

MERCUTIO   Good King of Cats, nothing but one of your
nine lives, that I mean to make bold withal, and
as you shall use me hereafter, dry-beat the rest of
the eight. Will you pluck your sword out of his
pilcher by the ears? Make haste, lest mine be
about your ears ere it be out.   83

TYBALT   I am for you.

ROMEO   Gentle Mercutio, put thy rapier up.

MERCUTIO   Come sir, your *passado*.

ROMEO   Draw Benvolio, beat down their weapons.
Gentlemen, for shame, forbear this outrage.
Tybalt, Mercutio, the Prince expressly hath
Forbid this bandying in Verona streets.   90
Hold Tybalt. Good Mercutio.

PETRUCHIO   Away Tybalt. [*Tybalt under Romeo's arm, thrusts
Mercutio in and flies*

As Tybalt and his companions make good their escape, we realise that Mercutio is fatally wounded. He is helped away but dies almost immediately.

sped: done for

a grave man: a play on words: (a) a serious man (not a joker as previously) (b) buried in a grave

braggart: boaster

by the book of arithmetic: in modern language 'by the book'. (Tybalt has all the technique, but there is no personality to the way he fences. The use of 'arithmetic' also suggests that Tybalt is rather calculating in his behaviour.)

And in my ... steel: weakened the courage in my personality. A pun on temper, which can mean (a) state of mind (b) the toughness of steel

aspired: ascended to

on moe ... depend: threatens more days

MERCUTIO   I am hurt.
A plague on both your houses, I am sped.
Is he gone and hath nothing?

BENVOLIO   What, art thou hurt?

MERCUTIO   Ay, ay, a scratch, a scratch, marry 'tis enough.
Where is my page? Go villain, fetch a surgeon.

                                         [*Exit Page*

ROMEO   Courage man, the hurt cannot be much.

MERCUTIO   No 'tis not so deep as a well, nor so wide as a
church-door; but 'tis enough, 'twill serve. Ask for
me tomorrow, and you shall find me a grave   100
man. I am peppered, I warrant, for this world. A
plague on both your houses! 'Zounds, a dog, a
rat, a mouse, a cat, to scratch a man to death!
A braggart, a rogue, a villain, that fights by the
book of arithmetic! Why the devil came you
between us? I was hurt under your arm.

ROMEO   I thought all for the best.

MERCUTIO   Help me into some house Benvolio,
Or I shall faint. A plague a both your houses!
They have made worms' meat of me. I have it,
And soundly too. Your houses!   111

                  [*Exeunt Mercutio and Benvolio*

ROMEO   This gentleman, the Prince's near ally,
My very friend, hath got this mortal hurt
In my behalf; my reputation stained
With Tybalt's slander. Tybalt that an hour
Hath been my cousin. O sweet Juliet,
Thy beauty hath made me effeminate,
And in my temper softened valour's steel.

                   Enter BENVOLIO

BENVOLIO   O Romeo, Romeo, brave Mercutio is dead.
That gallant spirit hath aspired the clouds,   120
Which too untimely here did scorn the earth.

ROMEO   This day's black fate on moe days doth depend,

**As Romeo realises what he has done, Tybalt returns.
Romeo attacks him frenziedly and kills him. Romeo
escapes and the citizens of Verona begin to
congregate.**

respective lenity: respectful leniency
fire-eyed … conduct: in place of mildness Romeo is going
    to behave with furious anger, eyes blazing.
consort: accompany
doom thee death: sentence you to death

1 The citizens run in, searching for Tybalt because they
    have heard of the death of Mercutio. Benvolio shows
    them his body and is arrested.

1

This but begins the woe others must end.   ✗

Enter TYBALT

BENVOLIO	Here comes the furious Tybalt back again.
ROMEO	He go in triumph, and Mercutio slain?
	Away to heaven respective lenity,
	And fire-eyed fury be my conduct now.
	Now Tybalt take the 'villain' back again
	That late thou gavest me, for Mercutio's soul
	Is but a little way above our heads, 130
	Staying for thine to keep him company.
	Either thou or I, or both, must go with him.
TYBALT	Thou wretched boy, that didst consort him here,
	Shalt with him hence.
ROMEO	This shall determine that.

[*They fight. Tybalt falls*

BENVOLIO	Romeo away, be gone.
	The citizens are up and Tybalt slain.
	Stand not amazed, the Prince will doom thee death,
	If thou art taken. Hence, be gone, away.
ROMEO	O I am fortune's fool!
BENVOLIO	Why dost thou stay?

[*Exit Romeo*

Enter CITIZENS

CITIZEN	Which way ran he that killed Mercutio? 140
	Tybalt, that murderer, which way ran he?
BENVOLIO	There lies that Tybalt.
CITIZEN	Up sir, go with me;
	I charge thee in the Prince's name obey.

Enter PRINCE, MONTAGUE, CAPULET, *their Wives and all*

PRINCE	Where are the vile beginners of this fray?

**The Prince questions Benvolio about what happened.
Benvolio describes the two fights.**

2 The Prince asks what happened and Benvolio begins
to explain that Tybalt having killed Mercutio was then
killed by Romeo.
3 Lady Capulet, distressed at the death of her relative
demands the death penalty.
4 At the Prince's request, Benvolio explains in detail
what happened: Romeo tried to avoid a fight by
speaking calmly to Tybalt. Tybalt would not listen and
fought with Mercutio. As Romeo tried to stop them,
Tybalt killed Mercutio and fled. Tybalt came back,
Romeo turned on him and killed him. Then Romeo
fled.

BENVOLIO   O noble Prince, I can discover all
The unlucky manage of this fatal brawl.
There lies the man, slain by young Romeo,
That slew thy kinsman, brave Mercutio.

L. CAPULET   Tybalt, my cousin. O my brother's child!
O Prince! O husband! O the blood is spilled   150
Of my dear kinsman! Prince, as thou art true,
For blood of ours shed blood of Montague.
O cousin, cousin!

PRINCE   Benvolio, who began this bloody fray?

BENVOLIO   Tybalt here slain, whom Romeo's hand did slay.
Romeo, that spoke him fair, bade him bethink
How nice the quarrel was, and urged withal
Your high displeasure. All this uttered
With gentle breath, calm look, knees humbly
  bowed,
Could not take truce with the unruly spleen   160
Of Tybalt deaf to peace, but that he tilts
With piercing steel at bold Mercutio's breast;
Who, all as hot, turns deadly point to point,
And with a martial scorn, with one hand beats
Cold death aside, and with the other sends
It back to Tybalt, whose dexterity
Retorts it. Romeo he cries aloud,
'Hold friends, friends part!' And swifter than his
  tongue,
His agile arm bears down their fatal points,
And 'twixt them rushes; underneath whose arm   170
An envious thrust from Tybalt hit the life
Of stout Mercutio, and then Tybalt fled;
But by and by comes back to Romeo,
Who had but newly entertained revenge,
And to it they go like lightning, for ere I
Could draw to part them, was stout Tybalt slain.
And as he fell, did Romeo turn and fly.
This is the truth, or let Benvolio die.

The Prince pronounces judgment: Romeo is banished and the two families are fined.

5 >

5 Lady Capulet says that Benvolio is a Montague and so cannot be trusted. Romeo killed Tybalt and so should now be condemned to death.

6 The Prince points out that Tybalt had already killed Mercutio before Romeo killed him.

6 >

7 Montague agrees that Romeo has only brought what the law would have required anyway: the death of Tybalt.

7 >

8 The Prince pronounces sentence: Romeo is to be banished from Verona. Mercutio was a member of the Prince's family, so both Capulets and Montagues will be heavily fined. If Romeo is found in Verona he will be executed.

8 >

ACTIVITIES

Keeping track

Act 2 scene 5

1 What is Juliet's mood as she waits for the Nurse?
2 How does the Nurse react when Juliet asks her what happened?
3 What is Juliet's response to this?

L. CAPULET   He is a kinsman to the Montague;
             Affection makes him false, he speaks not true. 180
             Some twenty of them fought in this black strife,
             And all those twenty could but kill one life.
             I beg for justice, which thou, Prince must give.
             Romeo slew Tybalt, Romeo must not live.

PRINCE   Romeo slew him, he slew Mercutio.
             Who now the price of his dear blood doth owe?

MONTAGUE   Not Romeo, Prince, he was Mercutio's friend;
             His fault concludes but what the law should end,
             The life of Tybalt.

PRINCE   And for that offence
             Immediately we do exile him hence.   190
             I have an interest in your hate's proceeding;
             My blood for your rude brawls doth lie a-
             bleeding.
             But I'll amerce you with so strong a fine,
             That you shall all repent the loss of mine.
             I will be deaf to pleading and excuses,
             Nor tears nor prayers shall purchase out abuses.
             Therefore use none. Let Romeo hence in haste,
             Else, when he 's found, that hour is his last.
             Bear hence this body, and attend our will.
             Mercy but murders, pardoning those that kill.
                                              [*Exeunt*

Act 2 scene 6

4 While Romeo and Friar Lawrence wait for Juliet to arrive,
   they experience contrasting moods. What are they?

Act 3 scene 1

5 At the beginning of Act 3 scene 1, Benvolio wants
   Mercutio to 'retire'. Why is this, and what is
   Mercutio's response?
6 What does Tybalt want, when he speaks to Benvolio
   and Mercutio?
7 Why is Mercutio killed?
8 How does Romeo react to the death of Mercutio?
   What is the Prince's sentence on Romeo?

Discussion

Act 2 scene 5

1 Why do you think the Nurse behaves in this way
   towards Juliet?
2 How would you have felt if you had been Juliet?

Act 3 scene 1

3 What is the impact of this scene, coming immediately
   after the two preceding scenes?
4 What actually causes the fight between Mercutio and
   Tybalt?
5 Exactly what happens to Romeo between the moment
   when Tybalt first speaks to him and the moment when
   he kills Tybalt?
6 Is the Prince's sentence fair?

Drama

Fight to the death.

In groups of four or five.
Imagine that a photographer happened to be present
before and during the fight. Create a series of
photographs (see page 263) to represent the following
moments from Act 3 scene 1:

- The entrance of Tybalt - line 37
- Mercutio thou consort'st with Romeo - 46
- Here's my fiddlestick - 49
- Peace be with you sir - 58
- Thou art a villain - 62
- Villain am I none - 65
- Be satisfied - 73
- O calm - 74
- Tybalt, you rat catcher - 76

and so on; you choose other moments.

Your photographs could easily become drawings to
display in your classroom.

Stop!

In groups of five

Imagine the Prince's men had been on hand to stop the
fight at crucial moments. Using hotseating techniques
(see page 262), you could be detectives interviewing the
three combatants as if they had been stopped after the
following lines :

- Mercutio after - 'Hold, Tybalt, good Mercutio' line 91
- Tybalt after - 'This shall determine that.' line 134
- Romeo after - 'Oh I am fortune's fool' line 139

Character

Character logs

Add to your Character logs for:
Juliet, Nurse, Romeo, Friar Lawrence, Mercutio,
Benvolio, Tybalt.

Mercutio

Look back over what you wrote about Mercutio after Act
2 scene 4. Do the events of Act 3 scene 1 change your

view of his character? Think about these points:
- His refusal to agree with Benvolio and withdraw.
- His attitude towards Tybalt and the way he treats him.
- His behaviour when he realises he is going to die.
- What he says about the Montagues and the Capulets.

Tybalt

1 Look at your Character log for Tybalt. You should have notes for these scenes:
- Act 1 scene 5
- Act 3 scene 1.
2 Think about what the other characters say about him, especially Mercutio in Act 2 scene 4, lines 6-36.
3 Think, too, about how other people react towards him, especially Capulet in Act 1 scene 5 and Mercutio in Act 3 scene 1.
4 Now write a description of his character.

Juliet impatiently awaits the arrival of Romeo.

Gallop apace ... lodging: Phoebus Apollo, the god of the sun, drove his chariot from east to west across the sky. His *steeds* were *fiery-footed:* Juliet urges them to gallop fast (*apace*) so that night will come and bring Romeo to her.

Phaeton: Apollo's son who was allowed to drive the chariot of the sun for one day but was not strong enough to control it and so the sun came too close to the earth.

if love be blind: Cupid, the god of love, was described in the myths as blind. This idea occurs more than once in the play.

Writing

Choose one of these writing topics.

1 Write the newspaper obituaries of Tybalt and Mercutio.
2 Verona Radio broadcasts a special report on the disturbances leading to the deaths of Mercutio and Tybalt. As part of it a reporter conducts a series of short interviews with eye-witnesses and people involved. Write the interviews with any three of the following:
Benvolio, Prince Escalus, Capulet, Lady Capulet, Montague, a Citizen.

Quiz

Complete these short quotations. Who said each one?

1 These _____ delights have violent _____.
2 A_____ on both your _____.
3 The clock struck _____ when I did send the _____.

SCENE **2**

Juliet's room in Capulet's mansion.
Enter JULIET *alone*

JULIET   Gallop apace, you fiery-footed steeds,
Towards Phoebus' lodging; such a wagoner
As Phaeton would whip you to the west,
And bring in cloudy night immediately.
Spread thy close curtain, love-performing night,
That runaway's eyes may wink, and Romeo
Leap to these arms, untalked of and unseen.
Lovers can see to do their amorous rites
By their own beauties; or if love be blind,
It best agrees with night. Come civil night,   10

Juliet speaks of the darkness of night as her friend, since it will bring her lover to her. The Nurse brings the rope ladder but Juliet is surprised to see her so upset. She asks what is the matter.

sober-suited matron: Juliet sees night as a mature woman dressed in sombre black clothes

learn: teach

lose a winning match: she will *lose* her virginity but *win* Romeo

Hood my ... mantle: a reference to training a young, untrained (*unmanned*) hawk. When it got excited, it *bated*, making its wings flutter excitedly (as the blood flutters excitedly in Juliet's cheeks). When this happened, the falconer had to *hood* it with a dark cover (*mantle*) until it got used to the company of a man and was *manned*.

strange: unfamiliar

Think true ... modesty: Consider the act of making love as the action of a chaste (pure) person who is really in love.

weraday: alas

undone: lost, ruined

envious: hostile

Thou sober-suited matron all in black,
And learn me how to lose a winning match,
Played for a pair of stainless maidenhoods.
Hood my unmanned blood bating in my cheeks,
With thy black mantle, till strange love grow bold,
Think true love acted simple modesty.
Come night, come Romeo, come thou day in night;
For thou wilt lie upon the wings of night,
Whiter than new snow upon a raven's back.
Come gentle night, come loving black-browed
  night,   20
Give me my Romeo, and when I shall die,
Take him and cut him out in little stars,
And he will make the face of heaven so fine,
That all the world will be in love with night,
And pay no worship to the garish sun.
O I have bought the mansion of a love,
But not possessed it, and, though I am sold,
Not yet enjoyed. So tedious is this day,
As is the night before some festival
To an impatient child that hath new robes   30
And may not wear them. O here comes my Nurse,

Enter NURSE *wringing her hands, with the ladder of
cords in her lap*

And she brings news, and every tongue that speaks
But Romeo's name, speaks heavenly eloquence.
Now Nurse, what news? What hast thou there?
    The cords
That Romeo bid thee fetch?

NURSE   Ay, ay, the cords.

JULIET   Ay me, what news? Why dost thou wring thy hands?

NURSE   Ah weraday, he's dead, he's dead, he's dead.
We are undone lady, we are undone.
Alack the day, he's gone, he's killed, he's dead.

JULIET   Can heaven be so envious?

The Nurse is so distressed that she cannot give Juliet a clear reply straightaway. At first Juliet is led to believe that it is Romeo who has been killed, but then the Nurse mentions Tybalt's name. At last Juliet discovers the truth: that Romeo has been banished for killing Tybalt.

Romeo can: The Nurse means that Romeo could be hostile to Tybalt because he killed him, but Juliet doesn't understand her (since she doesn't know what has happened).

'Ay' -'I' - eye: (these are all pronounced the same, of course.) In her wild state of mind, Juliet uses a complicated play on words. 'Ay' means 'yes', and was often, in Shakespeare's time, written 'I', a 'bare vowel'. The cockatrice was a mythical creature that could kill you with a look (with its 'eye'). Juliet says that if the answer is 'yes', then she is no longer herself because Romeo's death destroys her true personality. (And if the answer is 'Ay' that he is dead, then his 'eyes' are 'shut'.)

piteous corse: pitiful corpse

swounded: fainted

bankrupt: her heart has lost all its possessions and so is 'broke'.

Vile earth ... resign: she tells her body (vile earth) to die (so that it can be buried in the earth).

bier: the stretcher on which the dead body was carried

general doom: on the Day of Judgment the trumpet would sound and all souls called before God to be judged.

serpent: In *Genesis*, the Devil took the form of a snake to tempt Eve in the Garden of Eden.

flow'ring: handsome

NURSE   Romeo can,   40
                    Though heaven cannot. O Romeo, Romeo,
                    Who ever would have thought it? Romeo!

JULIET   What devil art thou that dost torment me thus?
                    This torture should be roared in dismal hell.
                    Hath Romeo slain himself? Say thou but 'Ay',
                    And that bare vowel 'I' shall poison more
                    Then the death-darting eye of cockatrice.
                    I am not I, if there should be such an 'I';
                    Or those eyes shut, that make thee answer 'Ay'.
                    If he be slain, say 'ay'; or if not, 'no'.   50
                    Brief sounds determine of my weal or woe.

NURSE   I saw the wound, I saw it with mine eyes-
                    God save the mark-here on his manly breast.
                    A piteous corse, a bloody piteous corse.
                    Pale, pale as ashes, all bedaubed in blood,
                    All in gore-blood. I swounded at the sight.

JULIET   O break, my heart, poor bankrupt, break at once.
                    To prison eyes, ne'er look on liberty.
                    Vile earth, to earth resign; end motion here;
                    And thou and Romeo press one heavy bier.   60

NURSE   O Tybalt, Tybalt, the best friend I had,
                    O courteous Tybalt, honest gentleman,
                    That ever I should live to see thee dead!

JULIET   What storm is this that blows so contrary?
                    Is Romeo slaughtered? And is Tybalt dead?
                    My dearest cousin, and my dearer lord?
                    Then dreadful trumpet, sound the general doom,
                    For who is living, if those two are gone?

NURSE   Tybalt is gone, and Romeo banished.
                    Romeo that killed him, he is banished.   70

JULIET   O God, did Romeo's hand shed Tybalt's blood?

NURSE   It did, it did, alas the day, it did!

JULIET   O serpent heart, hid with a flow'ring face!
                    Did ever dragon keep so fair a cave?

Juliet is distraught at her conflict of loyalties: she loves Romeo but he has killed her cousin. When the Nurse tries to comfort her by agreeing and criticising Romeo, Juliet turns on her.

Beautiful tyrant ... show: Juliet has two ideas in her mind:- (a) that the Devil was once an angel who rebelled against God and so was once beautiful (b) that Romeo appears beautiful but his beauty hides an evil soul (because he killed Tybalt). These are further examples of *oxymoron* (see Glossary).

Just: exact

bower the spirit ... flesh: house the soul of a devil in such a beautiful and apparently saintly body

perjured/forsworn/dissemblers: all words referring to people who have lied about the most important things in life

naught: nothing

aqua vitae: brandy

chide at: criticise

Back foolish...joy: she tells her tears to go back where they came from since they should be paying tribute to sadness and not, as they are, being shed for happiness (her happiness that Romeo is still alive)

Beautiful tyrant, fiend angelical,
Dove-feathered raven, wolvish ravening lamb,
Despised substance of divinest show,
Just opposite to what thou justly seem'st,
A damned saint, an honourable villain.
O nature, what hadst thou to do in hell,   80
When thou didst bower the spirit of a fiend
In mortal paradise of such sweet flesh?
Was ever book containing such vile matter
So fairly bound? O that deceit should dwell
In such a gorgeous palace!

NURSE   There's no trust,
No faith, no honesty in men; all perjured,
All forsworn, all naught, all dissemblers.
Ah, where's my man? Give me some aqua vitae.
These griefs, these woes, these sorrows make me old.
Shame come to Romeo.

JULIET   Blistered be thy tongue 90
For such a wish. He was not born to shame.
Upon his brow shame is ashamed to sit;
For 'tis a throne where honour may be crowned
Sole monarch of the universal earth.
O what a beast was I to chide at him!

NURSE   Will you speak well of him that killed your cousin?

JULIET   Shall I speak ill of him that is my husband?
Ah poor my lord, what tongue shall smooth thy
    name,
When I thy three-hours' wife have mangled it?
But wherefore villain didst thou kill my cousin?   100
That villain cousin would have killed my husband.
Back foolish tears, back to your native spring.
Your tributary drops belong to woe,
Which you mistaking offer up to joy.
My husband lives, that Tybalt would have slain,
And Tybalt's dead, that would have slain my
    husband.

Juliet is even more upset when she begins to realise
what Romeo's banishment means to her. The Nurse
says that she will go to Romeo, who is hiding at Friar
Lawrence's cell.

forget it fain: gladly forget it

Or, if sour … moved: Or if unhappiness has to have
    company why didn't the death of her mother or father
    (or both) follow on from Tybalt's? That would have
    been an ordinary ('modern') kind of grief.

with a rear-ward following: following on from

beguiled: cheated

maiden-widowed: made a widow before the wedding
    night

maidenhead: virginity

wot: know

All this is comfort, wherefore weep I then?
Some word there was, worser than Tybalt's death,
That murdered me. I would forget it fain;
But O it presses to my memory,   110
Like damned guilty deeds to sinners' minds.
'Tybalt is dead, and Romeo banished.'
That 'banished', that one word 'banished',
Hath slain ten thousand Tybalts. Tybalt's death
Was woe enough if it had ended there.
Or if sour woe delights in fellowship,
And needly will be ranked with other griefs,
Why followed not, when she said 'Tybalt's dead',
'Thy father', or 'thy mother', nay or both,
Which modern lamentation might have moved?   120
But with a rear-ward following Tybalt's death,
'Romeo is banished'-to speak that word,
Is father, mother, Tybalt, Romeo, Juliet,
All slain, all dead. 'Romeo is banished.'
There is no end, no limit, measure, bound,
In that word's death; no words can that woe sound.
Where is my father and my mother, Nurse?

NURSE   Weeping and wailing over Tybalt's corse.
Will you go to them? I will bring you thither.

JULIET   Wash they his wounds with tears? Mine shall be
spent,
When theirs are dry, for Romeo's banishment.   130
Take up those cords. Poor ropes you are beguiled,
Both you and I, for Romeo is exiled.
He made you for a highway to my bed,
But I a maid die maiden-widowed.
Come cords, come Nurse, I'll to my wedding-bed,
And death, not Romeo, take my maidenhead.

NURSE   Hie to your chamber. I'll find Romeo
To comfort you. I wot well where he is.
Hark ye, your Romeo will be here at night.   140
I'll to him, he is hid at Lawrence' cell.

Juliet sends her ring as a token and asks the Nurse to tell Romeo to come to her to say goodbye.

Friar Lawrence returns to his cell, where Romeo is hiding. He tells Romeo that the Prince's sentence is banishment from Verona. Romeo responds that since he will no longer be able to be with Juliet, it might as well be a death sentence.

fearful: frightened
Affliction ... calamity: Unhappiness has fallen in love with you, and you are married to disaster.
doom: sentence
What sorrow craves ... hand: What new unhappiness wants to get to know me?
death mis-termed: another name for death

JULIET   O find him, give this ring to my true knight,
               And bid him come to take his last farewell.

                                             [*Exeunt*

Friar Lawrence's cell.
Enter FRIAR LAWRENCE

F. LAWRENCE   Romeo come forth, come forth thou fearful man.
               Affliction is enamoured of thy parts,
               And thou art wedded to calamity.

               Enter ROMEO

ROMEO   Father what news? What is the Prince's doom?
               What sorrow craves acquaintance at my hand,
               That I yet know not.

F. LAWRENCE   Too familiar
               Is my dear son with such sour company.
               I bring thee tidings of the Prince's doom.

ROMEO   What less than doomsday is the Prince's doom?

F. LAWRENCE   A gentler judgment vanished from his lips,
               Not body's death, but body's banishment.   10

ROMEO   Ha, banishment? Be merciful, say 'death';
               For exile hath more terror in his look,
               Much more than death. Do not say 'banishment'.

F. LAWRENCE   Here from Verona art thou banished.
               Be patient, for the world is broad and wide.

ROMEO   There is no world without Verona walls,
               But purgatory, torture, hell itself.
               Hence banished is banished from the world,
               And world's exile is death. Then 'banished'   20
               Is death mis-termed. Calling death 'banished',

As Romeo speaks he becomes increasingly wild and repeats that he might as well be dead.

Thy fault ... death: according to our law, the penalty for what you have done is death.

rushed aside: pushed to one side

validity: value

carrion flies: flies that feed on dead flesh

vestal: virgin

still blush ... sin: his idea is that her lips blush when they touch (kiss) each other.

the damned ... hell: souls that are in hell are banished from the presence of God.

sin-absolver: his confessor who pronounces forgiveness of his sins

mangle: hack, cut repeatedly

1 The Friar tries to persuade Romeo to listen to reason.

	Thou cut'st my head off with a golden axe,
	And smilest upon the stroke that murders me.
F. LAWRENCE	O deadly sin! O rude unthankfulness!
	Thy fault our law calls death, but the kind Prince
	Taking thy part hath rushed aside the law,
	And turned that black word death to banishment.
	This is dear mercy, and thou seest it not.
ROMEO	'Tis torture and not mercy. Heaven is here
	Where Juliet lives, and every cat and dog, 30
	And little mouse, every unworthy thing,
	Live here in heaven, and may look on her,
	But Romeo may not. More validity,
	More honourable state, more courtship lives
	In carrion flies than Romeo. They may seize
	On the white wonder of dear Juliet's hand,
	And steal immortal blessing from her lips,
	Who even in pure and vestal modesty
	Still blush, as thinking their own kisses sin.
	But Romeo may not, he is banished. 40
	Flies may do this, but I from this must fly;
	They are free men, but I am banished.
	And sayest thou yet that exile is not death?
	Hadst thou no poison mixed, no sharp-ground knife,
	No sudden mean of death, though ne'er so mean,
	But 'banished' to kill me? Banished?
	O friar, the damned use that word in hell;
	Howling attends it. How hast thou the heart,
	Being a divine, a ghostly confessor,
	A sin-absolver, and my friend professed, 50
	To mangle me with that word banished?
F. LAWRENCE	Thou fond mad man, hear me a little speak.
ROMEO	O thou wilt speak again of banishment.
F. LAWRENCE	I'll give thee armour to keep off that word,
	Adversity's sweet milk, philosophy,
	To comfort thee though thou art banished.

Romeo continues to reject the Friar's advice. Their conversation is interrupted by someone knocking at the door.

2 >

2 Romeo refuses: the Friar cannot possibly understand his plight.

3 The Friar tries again. Romeo tells him that unless he were in his shoes he couldn't possibly say anything useful. He throws himself on the ground.

3 >

4 There is a knock on the door. Friar Lawrence tells Romeo to hide, but he stays where he is.

5 It is the Nurse.

4 >

5 >

ROMEO Yet 'banished'? Hang up philosophy,
Unless philosophy can make a Juliet,
Displant a town, reverse a prince's doom,
It helps not, it prevails not. Talk no more.   60

F. LAWRENCE O then I see that madmen have no ears.

ROMEO How should they when that wise men have no eyes?

F. LAWRENCE Let me dispute with thee of thy estate.

ROMEO Thou canst not speak of that thou dost not feel.
Wert thou as young as I, Juliet thy love,
An hour but married, Tybalt murdered,
Doting like me, and like me banished,
Then mightst thou speak, then mightst thou tear
  thy hair,
And fall upon the ground, as I do now,
Taking the measure of an unmade grave.   70

NURSE *knocks*

F. LAWRENCE Arise; one knocks; good Romeo hide thyself.

ROMEO Not I, unless the breath of heart-sick groans
Mist-like enfold me from the search of eyes.
[*Nurse knocks*

F. LAWRENCE Hark how they knock! Who's there?Romeo arise;
Thou wilt be taken-Stay awhile-Stand up.
                                    [*Nurse knocks*

Run to my study-By and by-God's will,
What simpleness is this? - I come, I come.   [*Nurse
                                             knocks*

Who knocks so hard? Whence come you? What's
  your will?

NURSE [*Within*] Let me come in, and you shall know my
  errand.
I come from Lady Juliet.

F. LAWRENCE   Welcome then.   80

NURSE O holy friar, O tell me holy friar,

The Nurse arrives to see Romeo collapsed on the floor in his unhappiness. She tells them that Juliet is similarly grief-stricken. On hearing this Romeo blames himself and tries to kill himself but they stop him.

6

7

6 The Nurse asks for Romeo and the Friar points to him on the ground.
7 She says that Juliet is in exactly the same state. She persuades him to get up.
8 Romeo asks after Juliet and is told that she is overcome with grief, weeping over the death of Tybalt and the banishment of Romeo.

8

9 Romeo blames himself for this and tries to stab himself. The Nurse stops him.

9

	Where is my lady's lord? Where's Romeo?
F. LAWRENCE	There on the ground, with his own tears
	made drunk.
NURSE	O he is even in my mistress' case,
	Just in her case. O woeful sympathy,
	Piteous predicament! Even so lies she,
	Blubbering and weeping, weeping and blubbering.
	Stand up, stand up; stand an you be a man.
	for Juliet's sake, for her sake rise and stand.
	Why should you fall into so deep an O? 90
ROMEO	Nurse-
NURSE	Ah sir, ah sir, death's the end of all.
ROMEO	Spakest thou of Juliet? How is it with her?
	Doth not she think me an old murderer,
	Now I have stained the childhood of our joy
	With blood removed but little from her own?
	Where is she? And how doth she? And what says
	My concealed lady to our cancelled love?
NURSE	O she says nothing sir, but weeps and weeps,
	And now falls on her bed, and then starts up,
	And Tybalt calls, and then on Romeo cries, 100
	And then down falls again.
ROMEO	As if that name,
	Shot from the deadly level of a gun,
	Did murder her, as that name's cursed hand
	Murdered her kinsman. O tell me friar, tell me,
	In what vile part of this anatomy
	Doth my name lodge? Tell me that I may sack
	The hateful mansion.

[*He offers to stab himself and the Nurse snatches the
dagger away*

	Hold thy desperate hand.
F. LAWRENCE	Art thou a man? Thy form cries out thou art.
	Thy tears are womanish, thy wild acts denote
	The unreasonable fury of a beast. 110
	Unseemly woman in a seeming man,

**Friar Lawrence tells him to get control of himself:
Juliet and he are both still alive.**

10>

11>

10 The Friar is horrified at this: suicide is the
   unforgivable sin and not worthy of a human being.
11 If Romeo kills himself he will kill Juliet, too. Why
   does he curse his own birth, and heaven and earth -
   because they all meet in his body that he has tried to
   kill?
12 By such an action he would sin against his own
   personality and the love he shares with Juliet.

12>

dead: wanting to die
would: wanted to
Happiness courts ... array: Happiness woos (makes up
   to) you all dressed in its best clothes.
mishaved: badly behaved
sullen wench: bad-tempered girl
such die miserable: people who behave in that way die
   unhappy.
decreed: arranged
the watch be set: at night the gates of the city were closed
   and the streets patrolled by watchmen. So Romeo could
   either leave freely before then, or early the following
   morning in disguise, as soon as the gates were opened
   again.

And ill-beseeming beast in seeming both,
Thou hast amazed me. By my holy order,
I thought thy disposition better tempered.
Hast thou slain Tybalt? Wilt thou slay thyself,
And slay thy lady that in thy life lives,
By doing damned hate upon thyself?
Why railest thou on thy birth, the heaven, and earth,
Since birth, and heaven, and earth, all three do
    meet
In thee at once; which thou at once wouldst lose? 120
Fie, fie, thou shamest thy shape, thy love, thy wit,
Which like a usurer abound'st in all,
And usest none in that true use indeed
Which should bedeck thy shape, thy love, thy wit.
Thy noble shape is but a form of wax,
Digressing from the valour of a man;
Thy dear love sworn but hollow perjury,
Killing that love which thou hast vowed to cherish.
Thy wit, that ornament to shape and love,
Misshapen in the conduct of them both, 130
Like powder in a skilless soldier's flask,
Is set afire by thine own ignorance,
And thou dismembered with thine own defence.
What, rouse thee man, thy Juliet is alive,
For whose dear sake thou wast but lately dead.
There art thou happy. Tybalt would kill thee,
But thou slewest Tybalt; there art thou happy.
The law that threatened death becomes thy friend,
And turns it to exile; there art thou happy.
A pack of blessings light upon thy back, 140
Happiness courts thee in her best array,
But like a mishaved and sullen wench,
Thou pouts upon thy fortune and thy love.
Take heed, take heed, for such die miserable.
Go get thee to thy love as was decreed,
Ascend her chamber, hence and comfort her.
But look thou stay not till the watch be set,

**Romeo must go to Mantua and wait until the
situation can be sorted out. The Nurse gives Romeo
Juliet's ring and they arrange that Romeo will spend
the night with Juliet but depart for Mantua before it is
light.**

blaze: make public
lamentation: grief
Which heavy ... unto: which they are likely to want to do
anyway because of their grief

1 The Nurse praises the Friar's advice and then prepares
to go, saying that she will tell Juliet that Romeo is on
his way.
2 She gives him Juliet's ring and then goes.
3 Romeo is encouraged by this.
4 The Friar explains to Romeo that he can either leave
Verona before nightfall or spend the night with Juliet
and go early in the morning in disguise. The Friar will
use Romeo's servant as a messenger to carry news of
what is happening in Verona. He bids him goodbye.
5 Romeo expresses sadness that their parting must be so
hurried and goes.

For then thou canst not pass to Mantua,
Where thou shalt live till we can find a time
To blaze your marriage, reconcile your friends, 150
Beg pardon of the Prince, and call thee back
With twenty hundred thousand times more joy
Than thou went'st forth in lamentation.
Go before Nurse, commend me to thy lady,
And bid her hasten all the house to bed,
Which heavy sorrow makes them apt unto.
Romeo is coming.

NURSE   O Lord, I could have stayed here all the night
to hear good counsel. O what learning is!
My lord, I'll tell my lady you will come.   160

ROMEO   Do so, and bid my sweet prepare to chide.
[Nurse offers to go in and turns again

NURSE   Here sir, a ring she bid me give you sir.
Hie you, make haste, for it grows very late. *[Exit*

ROMEO   How well my comfort is revived by this.

F. LAWRENCE   Go hence; good night; and here stands all your
state-
Either be gone before the watch be set,
Or by the break of day disguised from hence.
Sojourn in Mantua; I'll find out your man,
And he shall signify from time to time
Every good hap to you that chances here.   170
Give me thy hand, 'tis late. Farewell; good night.

ROMEO   But that a joy past joy calls out on me,
It were a grief, so brief to part with thee.
Farewell.   *[Exeunt*

Juliet's father, Capulet, tells Paris that he agrees to his marriage to Juliet. The ceremony shall take place two and a half days later, on Thursday. Lady Capulet will tell Juliet what they have decided.

1 Capulet tells Paris that because of the sadness they all feel about Tybalt's death he has not had time to persuade Juliet that she should marry him. It is too late that night for Paris to see her.

2 Paris accepts the situation and asks Lady Capulet to send Juliet his greetings.

3 As Paris is about to leave, Capulet calls him back and says he has decided that Juliet should marry him - she will obey his wishes. Lady Capulet should tell her that the ceremony will take place on Wednesday.

4 He changes his mind and settles on Thursday. He asks Paris if he is happy for the wedding to be celebrated so soon and with little ceremony, because of the death of Tybalt.

SCENE 4

Capulet's mansion
Enter CAPULET, LADY CAPULET, *and* PARIS

CAPULET   Things have fall'n out sir, so unluckily,
            That we have had no time to move our daughter.
            Look you, she loved her kinsman Tybalt dearly,
            And so did I. Well, we were born to die.
            'Tis very late, she'll not come down tonight.
            I promise you, but for your company,
            I would have been abed an hour ago.

PARIS   These times of woe afford no time to woo.
            Madam good night, commend me to your
                daughter.

L. CAPULET I will, and know her mind early tomorrow;   10
            Tonight she's mewed up to her heaviness.
                [Paris offers to go in and Capulet calls him again

CAPULET   Sir Paris, I will make a desperate tender
            Of my child's love. I think she will be ruled
            In all respects by me; nay more, I doubt it not.
            Wife, go you to her ere you go to bed,
            Acquaint her here of my son Paris' love;
            And bid her, mark you me, on Wednesday next-
            But soft, what day is this?

PARIS   Monday my lord.

CAPULET   Monday? Ha, ha, well Wednesday is too soon;
            A Thursday let it be a' Thursday, tell her,   20
            She shall be married to this noble earl.
            Will you be ready? Do you like this haste?
            We'll keep no great ado-a friend or two.
            For hark you, Tybalt being slain so late,
            It may be thought we held him carelessly,
            Being our kinsman, if we revel much.
            Therefore we'll have some half a dozen friends,
            And there an end. But what say you to Thursday?

5 Paris agrees.
6 Capulet bids him farewell and tells his wife to tell Juliet what they have decided.

5
6

ACTIVITIES

Keeping track

Act 3 scene 2

1 When does this scene take place?
2 What is Juliet's mood at the beginning of the scene?
3 How does the Nurse confuse Juliet?
4 How does Juliet react when she discovers what has happened?
5 What arrangement do they make at the end of the scene?

Act 3 scene 3

6 Friar Lawrence tells Romeo of his banishment from Verona. How does Romeo respond?
7 Why does Friar Lawrence tell Romeo to hide?
8 What is Romeo's reason for trying to kill himself?

Act 3 scene 4

9 When does this scene take place?
10 The Capulets change their minds twice in this scene. How and why?

PARIS   My lord, I would that Thursday were tomorrow.

CAPULET   Well get you gone; a' Thursday be it then.   30
Go you to Juliet ere you go to bed,
Prepare her, wife, against this wedding-day.
Farewell my lord. Light to my chamber ho!
Afore me, it is so very late that we
May call it early by and by. Good night. [*Exeunt*

Discussion

Dramatic irony

If you are not sure what this means, check in the
Glossary on page 286.

1 What emotions does Juliet express at the beginning of
   Act 3 scene 2?
2 How does she think of Romeo?
3 What do we know that she does not?
4 How does this affect the impact her first speech has on
   us?
5 During the confusion between Juliet and the Nurse,
   there is again something we know that Juliet doesn't.
   What is it and how does it affect our response to what
   happens?

Banishment and death

Look again at Act 3 scene 3. In particular look at how
Romeo responds to the news that he has been banished.

6 What does Romeo say about banishment and death?
7 If you were Romeo would you prefer death to
   banishment?

8 Do you think Romeo really means what he says? What makes you think this?

9 How helpful is Friar Lawrence in this situation?

10 Look at lines 149-53. Do you think Friar Lawrence really believes this - or is he just saying it?

Drama

Thou fond madman.

Groups of four or five.

It would be easy to dismiss Romeo as a spoilt, sulky and self-pitying young man. His speeches in the first half of Act 3 scene 3 up to when he tries to stab himself (line 109) do demonstrate a desperate madness. On stage an actor could use these speeches to whip himself into a frenzy of angry self-pity. Shakespeare provides the sounds and words for this.

1 Divide Romeo's lines between you and practise saying them out loud together.

2 Find those sounds and words which you can emphasise to 'whip up the frenzy'- paying particular attention to the word 'banishèd' (the accent indicates that we should pronounce the 'e' as in bed)

3 Look for examples of onomatopoeia and alliteration (see page 287 and page 286). Emphasise these. For example: doomsday, doom, death (repeated), golden axe, cat and dog, more ... more ... more, carrion flies, white wonder, flies ... fly, howling, how hast thou the heart, mangle me etc.

4 Try using menacing whispers and sudden pauses as well as loud and fierce sounds.

5 When you have had enough practice, each group should have a turn saying their lines out loud, one after the other.

6 Then use the lines as weapons. Each group tries to outdo the others - try to avoid just being louder - be

more subtle. Don't worry about saying the whole of your section, find those words and sounds which make the best weapons.

7 Finally a series of volunteers could become Romeo attacked by a chorus of his own words, turning this way and that, wringing his hands, flailing about, putting his hands over his ears in torment. Try building the frenzy up and down, alter the pace, making crescendos and finding out what silence does to him. All this should be done with a lot of action but there should be no physical contact.

Character

Hopes and fears

Take a piece of paper and divide it into three columns, headed:
Character, Hopes, Fears
For each of the characters in this section of the play make a list of their hopes and their fears at the end of Act 3 scene 4.

Romeo and Juliet

In rapid succession we are shown the reaction first of Juliet and then of Romeo to the news of Tybalt's death and Romeo's banishment. Think about these questions:

1 Do they both react in the same way?
2 If there are differences, what are they?
3 What do we learn about their characters from these two scenes?
4 Add to your Character logs for Romeo and Juliet.

The Nurse

5 Compare the way that the Nurse behaves when she is with these characters:

Juliet, Friar Lawrence, Romeo
Is she the same with all three, or are there differences?

6 Add to your Character log for the Nurse.

Other characters

7 Do you think Friar Lawrence gives Romeo the best possible advice?

8 Think about this and then add to your Character log for him.

9 Compare the behaviour of Capulet and Lady Capulet in Act 3 scene 4 with what they say in Act 1 scenes 2 and 3. Exactly how have they changed their position about Juliet's age, the possibility of her marrying Paris, and the need for her to agree to the marriage?

10 How does this affect your judgment of their characters?

11 Add to your Character logs for these two.

Close study

Act 3 scene 2 lines 1–31

1 Read this speech carefully, then close the book and write one or two sentences summing up what you think the speech is about.

2 Read the speech again. This time, write one or two sentences describing your feelings when you read (or hear) the speech.

3 How many times does the word 'night' occur in the speech?

4 What other words are used that refer to black and darkness?

5 The speech is an expression of Juliet's impatience to meet her lover and be alone with him for the first time since their marriage. What is the effect of all this emphasis on night and darkness?

6 Are there any other features of the speech that strike you as strange?

7 Now that you have thought about these points, has your reaction to the speech changed? If so, how?

It is almost light and Romeo is preparing to leave Juliet and travel to Mantua. Juliet tries to persuade him to stay, saying that it is still night and Romeo says he will accept her judgment and risk death. Juliet realises he was right before and tells him he must go.

fearful: apprehensive, worried about what is going to happen

yon: yonder, over there

envious: spiteful

jocund: happy

some meteor that ... exhaled: people believed that meteors were sucked up from the earth by the sun which then set them on fire.

ta'en: taken (said as one syllable, to rhyme with 'main')

so: if

the pale ... brow: the pale reflection of the forehead of Cynthia, goddess of the moon

vaulty: domed

Straining: forcing out (but also a pun on 'strain', meaning 'tune')

division: a run of musical notes (but also a pun - see the next line).

SCENE **5**

Juliet's bedroom
Enter ROMEO *and* JULIET *at the window*

JULIET   Wilt thou be gone? It is not yet near day.
            It was the nightingale, and not the lark,
            That pierced the fearful hollow of thine ear;
            Nightly she sings on yon pomegranate tree.
            Believe me love, it was the nightingale.

ROMEO   It was the lark, the herald of the morn,
            No nightingale. Look love, what envious streaks
            Do lace the severing clouds in yonder east.
            Night's candles are burnt out, and jocund day
            Stands tiptoe on the misty mountain tops.   10
            I must be gone and live, or stay and die.

JULIET   Yon light is not daylight, I know it, I.
            It is some meteor that the sun exhaled,
            To be to thee this night a torch-bearer,
            And light thee on thy way to Mantua.
            Therefore stay yet, thou need'st not to be gone.

ROMEO   Let me be ta'en, let me be put to death;
            I am content, so thou wilt have it so.
            I'll say yon gray is not the morning's eye,
            'Tis but the pale reflex of Cynthia's brow.   20
            Nor that is not the lark, whose notes do beat
            The vaulty heaven so high above our heads.
            I have more care to stay than will to go.
            Come death, and welcome, Juliet wills it so.
            How is't, my soul? Let's talk; it is not day.

JULIET   It is, it is, hie hence, be gone, away.
            It is the lark that sings so out of tune,
            Straining harsh discords, and unpleasing sharps.
            Some say the lark makes sweet division;

The Nurse warns them that Lady Capulet is coming and Romeo and Juliet say farewell. Romeo leaves.

Some say ... eyes: because a toad's eyes are more beautiful than a lark's

Since arm ... day: Since that noise startles us out of each other's arms, chasing you away with the morning call that wakes the hunters.

all these ... discourses: all these sadnesses will form the subject of our conversation.

ill-divining: fearing that something bad will happen in the future

now thou ... low: because Romeo has started climbing down the ladder.

Dry sorrow ... blood: people believed that sighing (for sorrow) thinned your blood and so made you pale.

	This doth not so, for she divideth us.	30
	Some say the lark and loathed toad changed eyes,	
	O now I would they had changed voices too,	
	Since arm from arm that voice doth us affray,	
	Hunting thee hence with hunt's-up to the day.	
	O now be gone; more light and light it grows.	
ROMEO	More light and light, more dark and dark our woes.	

Enter NURSE *hastily*

NURSE	Madam.
JULIET	Nurse.
NURSE	Your lady mother is coming to your chamber.
	The day is broke, be wary, look about. 40
	[*Exit*
JULIET	Then window let day in, and let life out.
ROMEO	Farewell, farewell. One kiss, and I'll descend.
	[*He goes down*
JULIET	Art thou gone so, love lord, ay husband, friend?
	I must hear from thee every day in the hour,
	For in a minute there are many days.
	O by this count I shall be much in years,
	Ere I again behold my Romeo.
ROMEO	Farewell.
	I will omit no opportunity
	That may convey my greetings, love, to thee. 50
JULIET	O think'st thou we shall ever meet again?
ROMEO	I doubt it not, and all these woes shall serve
	For sweet discourses in our times to come.
JULIET	O God, I have an ill-divining soul.
	Methinks I see thee now thou art so low,
	As one dead in the bottom of a tomb.
	Either my eyesight fails, or thou lookest pale.
ROMEO	And trust me love, in my eye so do you.
	Dry sorrow drinks our blood. Adieu, adieu. [*Exit*
JULIET	O fortune, fortune, all men call thee fickle; 60

Lady Capulet greets her daughter and asks her how she is. She sympathises with Juliet's grief at the death of Tybalt and her hatred of the villain Romeo.

What unaccustomed ... hither?: What unusual reason brings her here?

An if: even if

some grief ... wit: If you grieve a little it shows how much you loved (Tybalt); but if you grieve excessively it suggests that you are rather simple.

So shall ... for: If you do that you will experience the sense of loss but you won't bring back the friend you are grieving for.

Villain and he ... asunder: Romeo is very far from being a villain

And yet ... heart : And yet no man saddens me as much as he does.

Would none ... venge: I wish I were the only person to avenge.

If thou art fickle, what dost thou with him
That is renowned for faith? Be fickle, fortune;
For then I hope thou wilt not keep him long,
But send him back.   [*She goes down from the*
                                        window

Enter LADY CAPULET

L. CAPULET   Ho daughter, are you up?

JULIET   Who is't that calls? It is my lady mother.
Is she not down so late, or up so early?
What unaccustomed cause procures her hither?

L. CAPULET Why how now Juliet?

JULIET   Madam I am not well.

L. CAPULET Evermore weeping for your cousin's death?
What, wilt thou wash him from his grave with
          tears?   70
An if thou couldst, thou couldst not make him live.
Therefore have done; some grief shows much of
          love,
But much of grief shows still some want of wit.

JULIET   Yet let me weep for such a feeling loss.

L. CAPULET So shall you feel the loss, but not the friend
Which you weep for.

JULIET   Feeling so the loss,
I cannot choose but ever weep the friend.

L. CAPULET Well girl, thou weep'st not so much for his death,
As that villain lives which slaughtered him.

JULIET   What villain Madam?

L. CAPULET   That same villain Romeo. 80

JULIET   [*Aside*] Villain and he be many miles asunder-
God pardon him; I do with all my heart;
And yet no man like he doth grieve my heart.

L. CAPULET That is because the traitor murderer lives.

JULIET   Ay madam, from the reach of these my hands.
Would none but I might venge my cousin's death.

Juliet appears to agree with her mother's attack on
Romeo, but uses words that can also mean that she
loves Romeo. Lady Capulet then turns to the question
of marriage and tells Juliet to prepare to be married
to Paris in two days' time. Juliet is horrified and tells
her mother that she will do no such thing.

runagate: fugitive

unaccustomed dram: unexpected dose (of poison)

Indeed I ... vexed: Juliet's mother takes her to mean: 'I
never shall be satisfied with Romeo till I behold him
dead. My poor heart is so vexed for a kinsman (Tybalt).'
What she actually means is: 'I never shall be satisfied
with Romeo till I behold him. My poor heart is so vexed
for a kinsman (Romeo) that it is dead.'

temper: she means 'water it down', but her mother thinks
she means 'mix it up'.

O, how ... him: again she speaks with a double meaning.
She wants Romeo to be with her so that she can show
him her love. Lady Capulet assumes she means that she
wants to avenge herself on Romeo for Tybalt's death.

wreak: express

careful: thoughtful

L. CAPULET	We will have vengeance for it, fear thou not.
	Then weep no more. I'll send to one in Mantua,
	Where that same banished runagate doth live,
	Shall give him such an unaccustomed dram, 90
	That he shall soon keep Tybalt company
	And then I hope thou wilt be satisfied.
JULIET	Indeed I never shall be satisfied
	With Romeo, till I behold him-dead-
	Is my poor heart so for a kinsman vexed.
	Madam, if you could find out but a man
	To bear poison, I would temper it,
	That Romeo should upon receipt thereof
	Soon sleep in quiet. O how my heart abhors
	To hear him named-and cannot come to him-
	To wreak the love I bore my cousin 101
	Upon his body that hath slaughtered him.
L. CAPULET	Find thou the means, and I'll find such a man.
	But now I'll tell thee joyful tidings girl.
JULIET	And joy comes well in such a needy time.
	What are they, I beseech your ladyship?
L. CAPULET	Well, well, thou hast a careful father child,
	One who to put thee from thy heaviness
	Hath sorted out a sudden day of joy,
	That thou expects not, nor I looked not for. 110
JULIET	Madam, in happy time what day is that?
L. CAPULET	Marry my child, early next Thursday morn,
	The gallant, young and noble gentleman,
	The County Paris, at St Peter's Church,
	Shall happily make thee there a joyful bride.
JULIET	Now by Saint Peter's Church, and Peter too,
	He shall not make me there a joyful bride.
	I wonder at this haste, that I must wed
	Ere he that should be husband comes to woo.
	I pray you tell my lord and father, madam, 120
	I will not marry yet, and when I do, I swear
	It shall be Romeo, whom you know I hate,

Juliet's father enters, unaware of what Juliet has just said to her mother, and comments on his daughter's grief. His wife tells him that Juliet has refused to marry Paris. Capulet amazed to hear this and questions her about it. When she repeats her refusal Capulet loses his temper.

conduit: water pipe

counterfeit: represent

bark: boat

the winds ... body: The winds in his comparision are Juliet's sighs which blow as she weeps and unless there is a sudden calm they will capsize the boat (her body) which is being thrown about by the storm.

our decree: what we have decided.

she will none: she will have nothing to do with it.

take me with you: explain what you mean.

wrought: arranged

Not proud ... love: I am not proud of what you have done, but grateful to you (for the thought it shows). I can never be proud of something I hate but I can be grateful for something hateful if it was offered with love.

chopt logic: quibbling

minion: hussy

fettle your ...'gainst: prepare yourself for

I will ... hurdle: wrongdoers were often dragged through the streets on a piece of fencing pulled behind a horse

green-sickness carrion: he is saying that she looks as anaemic as a corpse

Rather than Paris. These are news indeed.

L. CAPULET   Here comes your father, tell him so yourself,
And see how he will take it at your hands.

Enter CAPULET *and* NURSE

CAPULET   When the sun sets, the earth doth drizzle dew;
But for the sunset of my brother's son
It rains downright.
How now, a conduit, girl? What, still in tears?
Evermore showering? In one little body   130
Thou counterfeits a bark, a sea, a wind.
For still thy eyes, which I may call the sea,
Do ebb and flow with tears; the bark thy body is
Sailing in this salt flood; the winds, thy sighs,
Who raging with thy tears, and they with them,
Without a sudden calm, will overset
Thy tempest-tossed body. How now wife,
Have you delivered to her our decree?

L. CAPULET   Ay sir, but she will none, she gives you thanks.
I would the fool were married to her grave.   140

CAPULET   Soft, take me with you, take me with you wife.
How will she none? Doth she not give us thanks?
Is she not proud? Doth she not count her blessed,
Unworthy as she is, that we have wrought
So worthy a gentleman to be her bride?

JULIET   Not proud you have, but thankful that you have.
Proud can I never be of what I hate,
But thankful even for hate, that is meant love.

CAPULET   How, how, how, how, chopt-logic. What is this?
'Proud', and 'I thank you', and 'I thank you not',   150
And yet 'not proud'. Mistress minion you,
Thank me no thankings, nor proud me no prouds,
But fettle your fine joints 'gainst Thursday next,
To go with Paris to Saint Peter's Church,
Or I will drag thee on a hurdle thither.
Out you green-sickness carrion, out you baggage,

Capulet tells Juliet that either she will marry Paris on
Thursday or he will disown her. The Nurse tries to
defend Juliet, only to be shouted down by Capulet,
who complains bitterly of Juliet's ingratitude.

baggage: hussy
tallow-face: white face
hilding: worthless child
Good prudence: Prudence may be the Nurse's name, but
　more likely Capulet is being sarcastic and telling her how
　'thoughtful' and 'sensible' she is.
smatter: chatter
God ye god-den: Goodbye - he means 'Be off with you!'
God's bread: he swears by the sacrament of the bread in
　the Mass.
matched: married
demesnes: estates
liened: descended
Stuffed, as ... parts: absolutely full of good qualities
puling: weeping
mammet: doll
in her ... tender: when by chance she receives a good offer
　(of marriage)

        You tallow-face!

L. CAPULET   Fie, fie, what, are you mad?

JULIET   Good father, I beseech you on my knees,
                              [She kneels down
      Hear me with patience, but to speak a word.

CAPULET   Hang thee young baggage, disobedient wretch!   160
      I tell thee what, get thee to church a Thursday,
      Or never after look me in the face.
      Speak not, reply not, do not answer me.
      My fingers itch. Wife, we scarce thought us blessed
      That God had sent us but this only child;
      But now I see this one is one too much,
      And that we have a curse in having her.
      Out on her, hilding!

NURSE   God in heaven bless her.
      You are to blame my lord to rate her so.

CAPULET   And why, my lady wisdom? Hold your tongue.   170
      Good prudence, smatter with your gossips, go.

NURSE   I speak no treason.

CAPULET   O God ye god-den.

NURSE   May not one speak?

CAPULET   Peace you mumbling fool.
      Utter your gravity o'er a gossip's bowl,
      For here we need it not.

L. CAPULET   You are too hot.

CAPULET   God's bread, it makes me mad.
      Day, night, hour, tide, time, work, play,
      Alone, in company, still my care hath been
      To have her matched; and having now provided
      A gentleman of noble parentage,   180
      Of fair demesnes, youthful and nobly liened,
      Stuffed as they say with honourable parts,
      Proportioned as one's thought would wish a man-
      And then to have a wretched puling fool,
      A whining mammet, in her fortune's tender,

Still in a towering rage at Juliet's rejection of all the loving attention she has recieved from her parents, Capulet storms off. Juliet speaks self-pityingly but receives no comfort from her mother who also leaves her. She turns to the Nurse for comfort in her predicament.

and: if

Graze: feed (he uses the word normally used for cows and other animals)

I do not use to jest: I am not accustomed to joking

advise: think about it.

acknowledge: recognise you as my daughter

bethink you: think about it.

I'll not be forsworn: I shall not change my mind.

that dim monument: the family vault

My husband ... earth?: Juliet means that when she married Romeo she gave a promise to heaven to be faithful to him. Until he dies and goes to heaven her promise will not be returned to her from heaven, freeing her to marry again.

practise stratagems: play tricks

all the world ... you: I'll bet you anything he won't dare come back to question your actions.

To answer 'I'll not wed, I cannot love,
I am too young, I pray you pardon me'–
But and you will not wed, I'll pardon you.
Graze where you will, you shall not house with me.
Look to't, think on't, I do not use to jest.   190
Thursday is near, lay hand on heart, advise.
And you be mine, I'll give you to my friend;
And you be not, hang, beg, starve, die in the streets,
For by my soul, I'll ne'er acknowledge thee,
Nor what is mine shall never do thee good.
Trust to't, bethink you, I'll not be forsworn.

                                                                    [Exit

JULIET   Is there no pity sitting in the clouds,
That sees into the bottom of my grief?
O sweet my mother cast me not away.
Delay this marriage for a month, a week,   200
Or if you do not, make the bridal bed
In that dim monument where Tybalt lies.

L. CAPULET Talk not to me, for I'll not speak a word.
Do as thou wilt, for I have done with thee.

                                                                    [Exit

JULIET   O God! O Nurse, how shall this be prevented?
My husband is on earth, my faith in heaven;
How shall that faith return again to earth,
Unless that husband send it me from heaven
By leaving earth? Comfort me, counsel me.
Alack, alack, that heaven should practise
    stratagems   210
Upon so soft a subject as myself!
What sayest thou, hast thou not a word of joy?
Some comfort, nurse.

NURSE   Faith here it is. Romeo
Is banished, and all the world to nothing,
That he dares ne'er come back to challenge you;
Or if he do, it needs must be by stealth.
Then since the case so stands as now it doth,

The Nurse advises Juliet to forget about Romeo and to marry Paris as her parents wish. Juliet asks her if that is what she really means and the Nurse says that it is. Juliet says that she accepts this advice; the Nurse is to tell her mother that she is sorry that she has upset her father and is going to see Friar Lawrence to make her confession. As soon as the Nurse has gone, Juliet expresses her true feelings about the Nurse's treachery. She will never confide in her again; instead she will go and ask Friar Lawrence's advice.

---

dishclout: dishcloth
Beshrew my very heart: May my heart be cursed if I am wrong, but
it excels: it is even better than
Amen: so be it, I agree.
Ancient damnation: wicked old woman
fiend: devil
forsworn: having broken my word
counsellor: adviser
Thou and ... twain: I will never confide in you again.

I think it best you married with the County.
O he's a lovely gentleman.
Romeo's a dishclout to him; an eagle, madam,   220
Hath not so green, so quick, so fair an eye
As Paris hath. Beshrew my very heart,
I think you are happy in this second match,
For it excels your first; or if it did not,
Your first is dead, or't were as good he were,
As living hence, and you no use of him.

JULIET Speak'st thou from thy heart?

NURSE   And from my soul too.
Or else beshrew them both.

JULIET   Amen.

NURSE   What?

JULIET Well thou hast comforted me marvellous much.
Go in, and tell my lady I am gone,   230
Having displeased my father, to Lawrence' cell,
To make confession, and to be absolved.

NURSE Marry I will, and this is wisely done.

                                                    [*Exit*

She looks after NURSE

JULIET Ancient damnation! O most wicked fiend!
Is it more sin to wish me thus forsworn,
Or to dispraise my lord with that same tongue
Which she hath praised him with above compare
So many thousand times? Go counsellor;
Thou and my bosom henceforth shall be twain.
I'll to the friar to know his remedy.   240
If all else fail, myself have power to die.   [*Exit*

ACTIVITIES

Keeping track

1 When does this scene take place?
2 In lines 1-25 Romeo and Juliet have a disagreement. What is it about and how 'serious' is it?
3 How would you describe Juliet's feelings at the moment of Romeo's departure?
4 How does Juliet trick her mother?
5 How does Juliet react to her mother's news of the planned wedding?
6 What is her father's *first* response to the news of her refusal?
7 How do his mood and attitude develop through the rest of the scene?
8 When Juliet's parents have gone, what is the Nurse's advice to Juliet?
9 How does Juliet respond to this and why does she do so?

Discussion

1 Look again at lines 1-64. Which group of two or three lines best sums up the feelings of (a) Romeo (b) Juliet about their parting?
2 In the conversation with her mother (lines 68-123), Juliet is clearly saying one thing and meaning another. Look at each of her speeches; for each one make up a 'thinks' speech which expresses what she is really thinking. Try reading the conversation, with two speakers playing the part of Juliet. One speaks the lines in the play, while the other speaks immediately afterwards and says her thoughts.
3 What is your reaction to the way in which Capulet

treats his daughter? Can you see any justification for it?

4 Work with the rest of the group to produce a collection of short quotations from this scene which sum up the drama and tension of the situation in which Romeo and Juliet find themselves. Either arrange your quotations to be spoken aloud by the group, or present them visually on a poster.

Drama

Family rows

In groups of four or five.

The four people in this row all have different views. Imagine after this scene that they all go their separate ways and meet other people. Improvise in small groups the animated conversations they would have recounting their version of the row. Put them in a modern setting. For example:

Capulet - at a gentleman's club, at a pub, on the golf course.

Lady Capulet - at the dressmaker's, out for lunch with friends, at the hairdressers.

Juliet - in the schoolyard, at a disco.

Nurse - in the kitchen, in the supermarket.

Character

Capulet

1 Study carefully Capulet's conversation with his daughter.

2 His attitude towards Juliet changes steadily throughout the scene. This is indicated in a number of ways. One is the words he uses to describe or address her. Make a list of them.

3 Compare this conversation with Act 1 scene 2 lines 8-19 and Act 3 scene 4 lines 1-14. What does this comparison tell you about Capulet?

4 Now add to your Character log.

Nurse

Compare the following short sections of the play, in which the Nurse appears:

Act 1 scene 3 lines 12-20, 60-62
Act 2 scene 4 lines 199-208
Act 2 scene 5 lines 21-78
Act 3 scene 2 lines 85-96, 128-143
Act 3 scene 5 lines 168-173, 213-233

Think about these questions:

1 What is her attitude to Juliet in each extract? (And what does she want for Juliet?)
2 Is she consistent?
3 Does her character change?
4 How do you judge her?

Juliet

Study these three short extracts from the scene:
lines 60-4, 116-123, 205-211, 234-241
How do you think Juliet has changed from the girl we met in Act 1 scene 3?

Close study

Lines 176-196

Groups of 3-4.
This speech is the climax of Capulet's anger with Juliet. It is a challenge for the actor and there are many different ways in which it can be performed. Take one or two sections each, dividing the speech like this:

● lines 176-179
● lines 179-187
● lines 188-191
● lines 192-196

Work on your own section:
- make sure that you understand clearly what it means;
- practise reading it aloud (quietly at first!) to get the rhythm of it;
- think about the louds and the softs in the section.

When you are all ready, try putting the speech together. Now you have to think about the pattern of the speech as a whole and work to make the different sections fit well together.

Writing

Choose one of these topics:

1 As you can imagine, the second part of this scene made a lot of noise in the Capulet household. All the servants were eager to know what was going on. Immediately afterwards Peter asks the Nurse what happened. Write their conversation as a script.

2 Immediately after they have left Juliet, her parents talk about what happened. Write their conversation as a script.

3 Make a poster to illustrate the situation that Juliet finds herself in. Place her at the centre with these characters in a circle round the outside:

Romeo, Capulet, Lady Capulet, the Nurse, Friar Lawrence, Paris.

Draw lines connecting her to each. At her end of each line write her thoughts and feelings about that character at the end of this scene. At the other end, write that character's thoughts and feelings.

Now use the information you have collected to write one or two paragraphs describing Juliet's predicament at the end of Act 3.

Count Paris tells Friar Lawrence that Capulet has decided that his wedding to Juliet should be on Thursday. Although this is very soon after the funeral of Tybalt it will help to ease Juliet's grief. Juliet and Paris meet. Paris tries to persuade her to think of him as her future husband but Juliet rebuffs him.

1 The Friar and Paris are speaking as the scene begins. Paris has just told him that the wedding has been arranged for Thursday. The Friar finds this rather short notice, but Paris says that this is what Capulet wants.

2 Friar Lawrence objects that Paris has not even got Juliet's agreement yet.

3 Paris says this is because of her great grief at Tybalt's death. Nevertheless the wedding may help her to get over it, or so her father thinks.

4 As the Friar is wondering how to slow things down, he sees Juliet approaching.

5 Paris greets her as his wife-to-be and Juliet snubs him.

6 Paris asks if she has come to make confession. If so she must confess she loves him. Juliet again keeps him at a distance.

Act four

Friar Lawrence's cell
Enter FRIAR LAWRENCE *and* PARIS

F. LAWRENCE	On Thursday sir? The time is very short.
PARIS	My father Capulet will have it so,
	And I am nothing slow to slack his haste.
F. LAWRENCE	You say you do not know the lady's mind?
	Uneven is the course, I like it not.
PARIS	Immoderately she weeps for Tybalt's death,
	And therefore have I little talked of love,
	For Venus smiles not in a house of tears.
	Now sir, her father counts it dangerous
	That she do give her sorrow so much sway; 10
	And in his wisdom hastes our marriage,
	To stop the inundation of her tears;
	Which too much minded by herself alone,
	May be put from her by society.
	Now do you know the reason of this haste.
F. LAWRENCE	[*Aside*] I would I knew not why it should be slowed.
	Look sir, here comes the lady towards my cell.

Enter JULIET

PARIS	Happily met, my lady and my wife.
JULIET	That may be sir, when I may be a wife.
PARIS	That 'may be' must be, love, on Thursday next. 20
JULIET	What must be shall be.
F. LAWRENCE	That's a certain text.
PARIS	Come you to make confession to this father?
JULIET	To answer that, I should confess to you.
PARIS	Do not deny to him that you love me.

When Paris leaves, Juliet begs Friar Lawrence to help her. If he cannot she is determined to kill herself rather than be married to Paris.

7 Paris tries again, this time commenting that she has been crying a lot and it spoils her face. Juliet retorts that it wasn't much to look at in the first place.

8 She cuts through the conversation by asking the Friar if he is free to hear her confession. He agrees.

9 Paris takes his leave and goes.

10 Juliet asks Friar Lawrence for his sympathy.

11 The Friar tells her that he knows what has happened. She is to be married to Paris on Thursday.

resolution: decision
presently: straight away
And ere ... deed: In the wedding ceremony her hand and Romeo's were joined together to symbolise their marriage, as the seal on a document shows it is genuine. Juliet does not want her hand to be the seal ('label') for a second marriage contract.

JULIET	I will confess to you that I love him.
PARIS	So will ye, I am sure, that you love me.
JULIET	If I do so, it will be of more price,
	Being spoke behind your back, than to your face.
PARIS	Poor soul, thy face is much abused with tears.
JULIET	The tears have got small victory by that, 30
	For it was bad enough before their spite.
PARIS	Thou wrong'st it more than tears with that report.
JULIET	That is no slander sir, which is a truth,
	And what I spake, I spake it to my face.
PARIS	Thy face is mine, and thou hast slandered it.
JULIET	It may be so, for it is not mine own.
	Are you at leisure holy father now,
	Or shall I come to you at evening mass?
F. LAWRENCE	My leisure serves me pensive daughter now.
	My lord, we must entreat the time alone. 40
PARIS	God shield I should disturb devotion.
	Juliet, on Thursday early will I rouse ye.
	Till then adieu, and keep this holy kiss. [*Exit*
JULIET	O shut the door, and when thou hast done so,
	Come weep with me, past hope, past cure, past help.
F. LAWRENCE	O Juliet I already know thy grief,
	It strains me past the compass of my wits.
	I hear thou must, and nothing may prorogue it,
	On Thursday next be married to this County.
JULIET	Tell me not friar, that thou hearest of this, 50
	Unless thou tell me how I may prevent it.
	If in thy wisdom thou canst give no help,
	Do thou but call my resolution wise,
	And with this knife I'll help it presently.
	God joined my heart and Romeo's, thou our hands;
	And ere this hand, by thee to Romeo's sealed,
	Shall be the label to another deed,
	Or my true heart with treacherous revolt
	Turn to another, this shall slay them both.

The Friar says that if she is prepared to face death, then he has a remedy that may work. He tells her to pretend to agree to the marriage. Then, the night before the wedding, she must take the potion he gives her.

---

extremes: desperate situation

arbitrating that ... bring: sorting out the problem which all your experience could not honourably solve.

If what...remedy: If what you say does not offer a solution

Which craves ... prevent: which demands an action as extreme and ruthless as we are trying to prevent.

Then is it ... from it: Then you, who are prepared to face death itself to escape from the shame of marrying Paris, are likely to be prepared to suffer something like death in order to avoid it.

charnel house: a small building near a church where human bones were stored. When the bodies of the dead had been buried for some years, the graves were sometimes dug up and the bones placed in the charnel house.

reeky shanks: shinbones full of rank-smelling moisture

chapless: without a lower jaw

unstained: pure

vial: small bottle or flask

distilling liquor: liquid that will penetrate the body

Therefore out of thy long-experienced time,   60
Give me some present counsel, or behold
'Twixt my extremes and me this bloody knife
Shall play the umpire, arbitrating that
Which the commission of thy years and art
Could to no issue of true honour bring.
Be not so long to speak; I long to die,
If what thou speak'st speak not of remedy.

F. LAWRENCE   Hold daughter, I do spy a kind of hope,
Which craves as desperate an execution,
As that is desperate which we would prevent.   70
If, rather than to marry County Paris,
Thou hast the strength of will to slay thyself,
Then is it likely thou wilt undertake
A thing like death to chide away this shame,
That cop'st with death himself to 'scape from it;
And if thou darest, I'll give thee remedy.

JULIET   O bid me leap, rather than marry Paris,
From off the battlements of any tower;
Or walk in thievish ways; or bid me lurk
Where serpents are; chain me with roaring
    bears;   80
Or hide me nightly in a charnel-house,
O'er-covered quite with dead men's rattling bones,
With reeky shanks and yellow chapless skulls;
Or bid me go into a new-made grave,
And hide me with a dead man in his shroud;
–Things that to hear them told have made me
    tremble–
And I will do it without fear or doubt,
To live an unstained wife to my sweet love.

F. LAWRENCE   Hold then, go home, be merry, give consent
To marry Paris. Wednesday is tomorrow;   90
Tomorrow night look that thou lie alone,
Let not the nurse lie with thee in thy chamber.
Take thou this vial, being then in bed,
And this distilling liquor drink thou off;

The potion will send her to sleep and make it look as if she is dead. She will be taken to the family vault where she will eventually wake up. Meanwhile the Friar will alert Romeo who will come to her there and take her to Mantua. Juliet agrees to this plan and hurries home with the drug.

humour: body fluid
keep his native progress: beat in the normal way
surcease: stop
testify: show that
wanned: pale
eyes' windows: eyelids
supple government: mobility
In thy best ... bier: the body dressed in her finest clothes carried in an open coffin
borne: carried
In the mean time ... drift: Meanwhile Romeo will know what we have done by letter, in preparation for the moment when you wake up again
toy: silly idea
Abate thy ... it: reduce your courage to carry it out
prosperous: successful
strength shall ... afford: and strength give me the help I need

When presently through all thy veins shall run
A cold and drowsy humour; for no pulse
Shall keep his native progress, but surcease;
No warmth, no breath, shall testify thou livest;
The roses in thy lips and cheeks shall fade
To wanned ashes; thy eyes' windows fall,   100
Like death when he shuts up the day of life.
Each part deprived of supple government,
Shall stiff and stark and cold appear like death,
And in this borrowed likeness of shrunk death
Thou shalt continue two and forty hours,
And then awake as from a pleasant sleep.
Now when the bridegroom in the morning comes
To rouse thee from thy bed, there art thou dead.
Then as the manner of our country is,
In thy best robes uncovered on the bier,   110
Thou shalt be borne to that same ancient vault,
Where all the kindred of the Capulets lie.
In the mean time, against thou shalt awake,
Shall Romeo by my letters know our drift,
And hither shall he come; and he and I
Will watch thy waking, and that very night
Shall Romeo bear thee hence to Mantua.
And this shall free thee from this present shame,
If no inconstant toy nor womanish fear
Abate thy valour in the acting it.   120

JULIET	Give me, give me. O tell not me of fear.
F. LAWRENCE	Hold. Get you gone, be strong and prosperous
	In this resolve. I'll send a friar with speed
	To Mantua, with my letters to thy lord.
JULIET	Love give me strength, and strength shall help
	afford.
	Farewell dear father. [*Exeunt*

Capulet is busying himself making preparations for the wedding; sending out invitations and hiring cooks. Juliet returns from her visit to Friar Lawrence and immediately asks her father to forgive her for her earlier behaviour.

1 Capulet sends one servant to invite the wedding guests and another to hire twenty cooks to prepare the feast.

2 He asks if Juliet has gone to Friar Lawrence and says he hopes that the visit will make her see sense.

headstrong: self-willed girl
gadding: wandering off to
behests: instructions, commands
enjoined: made to promise
prostrate: face down on the ground (to humble herself before her father)
knot knit up: business tied up
becomed: suitable, proper

SCENE 2

Capulet's mansion
Enter CAPULET, LADY CAPULET, NURSE, *and Servants*

CAPULET   So many guests invite as here are writ.
                                    [*Exit First Servant*
               Sirrah, go hire me twenty cunning cooks.
2ND SERVANT You shall have none ill sir, for I'll try if they can
               lick their fingers.
CAPULET   How canst thou try them so?
2ND SERVANT Marry sir, 'tis an ill cook that cannot lick his own
               fingers; therefore he that cannot lick his fingers
               goes not with me.
CAPULET   Go, be gone.   [*Exit*
               We shall be much unfurnished for this time.   10
               What, is my daughter gone to Friar Lawrence?
NURSE   Ay forsooth.
CAPULET   Well, he may chance to do some good on her;
               A peevish self-willed harlotry it is.
NURSE   See where she comes from shrift with merry look.

               Enter JULIET

CAPULET   How now my headstrong, where have you been
               gadding?
JULIET   Where I have learned me to repent the sin
               Of disobedient opposition
               To you and your behests, and am enjoined
               By holy Lawrence to fall prostrate here,   20
               To beg your pardon. Pardon I beseech you,
               Henceforward I am ever ruled by you.
CAPULET   Send for the County, go tell him of this.
               I'll have this knot knit up tomorrow morning.
JULIET   I met the youthful lord at Lawrence' cell,
               And gave him what becomed love I might,
               Not stepping o'er the bounds of modesty.

Capulet is delighted and decides that the wedding shall be a day earlier, on the Wednesday rather than the Thursday. Juliet and the Nurse go off to prepare for the wedding.

ornaments: clothes
Thursday: Lady Capulet still thinks that the wedding should be on the Thursday
tomorrow: her husband overrules her
We shall ... provision: We shan't be ready in time
warrant: promise, guarantee
What, ho! ... forth: He calls for one of the servants and then remembers he has sent them all off on errands.
Since this ... reclaimed: Since this self-willed girl has changed her ways

Juliet asks the Nurse to leave her as she wishes to spend the night on her own.

attires: clothes
orisons: prayers
cross: perverse

CAPULET   Why I am glad on't; this is well. Stand up.
This is as 't should be. Let me see the County.
Ay marry go, I say, and fetch him hither.   30
Now afore God, this reverend holy friar,
All our whole city is much bound to him.

JULIET   Nurse, will you go with me into my closet,
To help me sort such needful ornaments
As you think fit to furnish me tomorrow?

L. CAPULET   No, not till Thursday, there is time enough.

CAPULET   Go nurse, go with her; we'll to church tomorrow.
              [*Exeunt Juliet and Nurse*

L. CAPULET   We shall be short in our provision;
'Tis now near night.

CAPULET   Tush, I will stir about,
And all things shall be well, I warrant thee wife.   40
Go thou to Juliet, help to deck up her;
I'll not to bed tonight, let me alone.
I'll play the housewife for this once. What ho!
They are all forth. Well, I will walk myself
To County Paris, to prepare up him
Against tomorrow. My heart is wondrous light,
Since this same wayward girl is so reclaimed.
              [*Exeunt*

SCENE 3

Juliet's bedroom
JULIET *and* NURSE

JULIET   Ay, those attires are best; but gentle Nurse,
I pray thee leave me to myself tonight;
For I have need of many orisons,
To move the heavens to smile upon my state,
Which well thou knowest is cross and full of sin.

Juliet says goodnight to her mother and then is left alone. She takes out the drug which the Friar has given her and immediately begins to have doubts: perhaps it won't work; perhaps it is really a poison because the Friar wants her dead to save his reputation.

---

culled such ... tomorrow: collected together all the things we need for tomorrow

Subtly hath ministered: has secretly given me

Lest: in case

Tried: proved by experience to be

Redeem: rescue

The horrible ... night: Juliet is thinking of the effects that darkness and the nearness of so many dead bodies will have on her imagination ('conceit')

Enter LADY CAPULET

L. CAPULET	What, are you busy, ho? Need you my help?
JULIET	No madam, we have culled such necessaries
	As are behoveful for our state tomorrow.
	So please you, let me now be left alone,
	And let the Nurse this night sit up with you; 10
	For I am sure you have your hands full all,
	In this so sudden business.
L. CAPULET	Good night.
	Get thee to bed and rest, for thou hast need.

                        [*Exeunt Lady Capulet and Nurse*

JULIET	Farewell. God knows when we shall meet again.
	I have a faint cold fear thrills through my veins,
	That almost freezes up the heat of life.
	I'll call them back again to comfort me.
	Nurse! What should she do here?
	My dismal scene I needs must act alone.
	Come vial. 20
	What if this mixture do not work at all?
	Shall I be married then tomorrow morning?
	No, no, this shall forbid it. Lie thou there.

                        [*Lays down a dagger*

What if it be a poison which the friar
Subtly hath ministered to have me dead,
Lest in this marriage he should be dishonoured,
Because he married me before to Romeo?
I fear it is, and yet methinks it should not,
For he hath still been tried a holy man.
How if when I am laid into the tomb,   30
I wake before the time that Romeo
Come to redeem me? There's a fearful point.
Shall I not then be stifled in the vault,
To whose foul mouth no healthsome air breathes in,
And there die strangled ere my Romeo comes?
Or if I live, is it not very like,
The horrible conceit of death and night,

She puts these thoughts to one side, only to be assailed by other fears: of suffocation in the tomb and of going mad with fear when she wakes up. At last Juliet overcomes her doubts and swallows the liquid.

mandrake: a plant with a forked root that, because it resembled the shape of a human body, was believed to shriek when pulled out of the ground
distraught: driven mad
Environed with: surrounded by

In the Capulets' house everyone is busy making last-minute preparations for the wedding.

1 Lady Capulet and the Nurse are organising the preparation of food.
2 Capulet, too, is giving orders about food, and telling people to hurry up.

Together with the terror of the place–
As in a vault, an ancient receptacle,
Where for this many hundred years the bones   40
Of all my buried ancestors are packed,
Where bloody Tybalt yet but green in earth
Lies festering in his shroud, where as they say,
At some hours in the night spirits resort–
Alack, alack, is it not like that I,
So early waking–what with loathsome smells,
And shrieks like mandrakes' torn out of the earth,
That living mortals hearing them, run mad–
O if I wake, shall I not be distraught,
Environed with all these hideous fears,   50
And madly play with my forefathers' joints,
And pluck the mangled Tybalt from his shroud,
And in this rage, with some great kinsman's bone,
As with a club, dash out my desperate brains?
O look, methinks I see my cousin's ghost
Seeking out Romeo that did spit his body
Upon a rapier's point–stay Tybalt, stay!
Romeo! Romeo! Romeo! I drink to thee.
[*She falls upon her bed within the curtains*

SCENE 4

A room in Capulet's mansion
Enter LADY CAPULET *and* NURSE *with herbs*

L. CAPULET   Hold, take these keys, and fetch more spices, Nurse.

NURSE   They call for dates and quinces in the pastry.

Enter OLD CAPULET

CAPULET   Come, stir, stir, stir, the second cock hath crowed,
The curfew bell hath rung, 'tis three o'clock.
Look to the baked meats, good Angelica.

Capulet is rushing around getting in everyone's way and thoroughly enjoying himself.

3 The Nurse and his wife tell him to get out of their way and leave things to them.
4 Capulet continues to bustle about. He sends for more firewood.
5 He hears the music which announces the arrival of Paris and sends the Nurse to wake Juliet.

Spare not for cost.

NURSE   Go you cot-quean, go,
Get you to bed; faith you'll be sick tomorrow
For this night's watching.

CAPULET   No, not a whit; what, I have watched ere now
All night for lesser cause, and ne'er been sick.   10

L. CAPULET   Ay you have been a mouse-hunt in your time,
But I will watch you from such watching now.
                              [*Exeunt Lady Capulet and Nurse*

CAPULET   A jealous hood, a jealous hood.

*Enter three or four Serving-men, with spits, and logs,
and baskets*

                              Now fellow,

What is there?

SERVING-MAN Things for the cook sir, but I know not what.

CAPULET   Make haste, make haste. Sirrah fetch drier logs.
Call Peter, he will show thee where they are.

SERVING-MAN I have a head sir, that will find out logs,
And never trouble Peter for the matter.   [*Exit*

CAPULET   Mass and well said, a merry whoreson, ha!   20
Thou shalt be logger-head. Good faith, 'tis day.
The County will be here with music straight,
For so he said he would. I hear him near.
                              [*Music within*

Nurse! Wife! What ho! What, Nurse I say!

Enter NURSE

Go waken Juliet, go and trim her up.
I'll go and chat with Paris. Hie, make haste,
Make haste; the bridegroom he is come already.
Make haste I say.   [*Exeunt*

The Nurse goes to wake Juliet. At first she thinks she is very soundly asleep but gradually she realises that she is dead. Lady Capulet and her husband enter the bedroom and are horrified at this news.

slug-a-bed: sluggard, lazybones

take your pennyworths now: get what little bits of sleep you can now

hath set ... little: has put all his money (as in a game of cards) on it that you won't get much sleep tomorrow night

weraday: alas

aqua vitae: brandy

SCENE 5

Juliet's bedroom

NURSE   Mistress! What, mistress! Juliet! Fast, I warrant
              her. She–
         Why lamb, why lady–fie you slug-a-bed!
         Why love I say! Madam! Sweet-heart! Why bride!
         What, not a word? You take your pennyworths now.
         Sleep for a week; for the next night I warrant
         The County Paris hath set up his rest
         That you shall rest but little. God forgive me.
         Marry, and amen. How sound is she asleep!
         I must needs wake her. Madam, madam, madam!
         Ay, let the County take you in your bed,   10
         He'll fright you up i' faith. Will it not be?
                              [*Draws back the curtains*
         What, dressed, and in your clothes, and down again?
         I must needs wake you. Lady, lady, lady!
         Alas, alas, help, help, my lady's dead!
         O weraday that ever I was born!
         Some aqua vitae ho! My lord! My lady!

Enter LADY CAPULET

L. CAPULET   What noise is here?
NURSE   O lamentable day!
L. CAPULET   What is the matter?
NURSE   Look, look. O heavy day!
L. CAPULET   O me, O me, my child, my only life.
              Revive, look up, or I will die with thee.   20
              Help, help! Call help.

Enter CAPULET

CAPULET   For shame, bring Juliet forth; her lord is come.
NURSE   She's dead, deceased, she's dead, alack the day!

The Friar and Paris also arrive and are equally distressed. All five grieve the sudden and shattering death of Juliet. Friar Lawrence tries to calm their grief.

ta'en her hence: taken her away
deflowered by him: lost her virginity to him
In lasting ... pilgrimage: through all the hard work of his journey
solace: take comfort
catched: snatched
Beguiled: tricked

L. CAPULET	Alack the day, she's dead, she's dead, she's dead!
CAPULET	Ha! Let me see her. Out alas she's cold,
	Her blood is settled, and her joints are stiff;
	Life and these lips have long been separated.
	Death lies on her like an untimely frost
	Upon the sweetest flower of all the field.
NURSE	O lamentable day!
L. CAPULET	O woeful time! 30
CAPULET	Death that hath ta'en her hence to make me wail,
	Ties up my tongue, and will not let me speak.

Enter FRIAR LAWRENCE, PARIS *and Musicians*

F. LAWRENCE	Come, is the bride ready to go to church?
CAPULET	Ready to go, but never to return.
	O son, the night before thy wedding-day
	Hath death lain with thy wife; there she lies,
	Flower as she was, deflowered by him.
	Death is my son-in-law, death is my heir,
	My daughter he hath wedded. I will die,
	And leave him all; life, living, all is death's. 40
PARIS	Have I thought long to see this morning's face,
	And doth it give me such a sight as this?
L. CAPULET	Accursed, unhappy, wretched, hateful day,
	Most miserable hour that e'er time saw
	In lasting labour of his pilgrimage!
	But one, poor one, one poor and loving child,
	But one thing to rejoice and solace in,
	And cruel death hath catched it from my sight.
NURSE	O woe! O woeful, woeful, woeful day!
	Most lamentable day, most woeful day, 50
	That ever, ever, I did yet behold!
	O day! O day! O day! O hateful day!
	Never was seen so black a day as this.
	O woeful day! O woeful day!
PARIS	Beguiled, divorced, wronged, spited, slain,

Friar Lawrence tells them to remember that human beings are born to die and go to heaven, so that they should be happy that Juliet is now in heaven. Capulet accepts his words and says that the wedding they had planned will now be transformed into a funeral.

Uncomfortable: Refusing to give us comfort

solemnity: celebration

Confusion: disaster

Heaven and ... maid: You only shared your daughter with Heaven

her promotion: that she should do well

be advanced: get on in life

O, in this ... well: In this way of showing your love, you actually love her so badly that it drives you mad to see she is dead.

She's not ... young: The woman who is married for a long time does not have a good marriage; the woman who dies young has the best marriage. (The Friar is taking rather an extreme religious view: if a woman dies young she has less chance to sin and goes to heaven. The Friar knows that Juliet isn't really dead and this might account for his 'callousness', but then we know from the Prologue that Juliet will die young.)

stick your rosemary ... corse: rosemary, the herb that stood for remembrance, was used both at weddings and at funerals.

Yet nature's ... merriment: but common sense (which knows better) laughs at the tears which human nature makes us shed - because Juliet is in heaven.

All things ... funeral: Everything that we ordered to celebrate the wedding must now be transformed into what we need to mark a funeral.

melancholy: sad, gloomy

solemn hymns: hymns to celebrate the wedding

sullen dirges: gloomy music (for the funeral)

contrary: opposite

       Most detestable death, by thee beguiled,
       By cruel, cruel thee quite overthrown.
       O love! O life! Not life, but love in death.

CAPULET   Despised, distressed, hated, martyred, killed;
       Uncomfortable time, why cam'st thou now   60
       To murder, murder our solemnity?
       O child! O child! My soul and not my child.
       Dead art thou, alack my child is dead,
       And with my child my joys are buried.

F. LAWRENCE Peace ho, for shame! Confusion's cure lives not
       In these confusions. Heaven and yourself
       Had part in this fair maid, now heaven hath all,
       And all the better is it for the maid.
       Your part in her you could not keep from death,
       But heaven keeps his part in eternal life.   70
       The most you sought was her promotion,
       For 'twas your heaven she should be advanced;
       And weep ye now, seeing she is advanced
       Above the clouds, as high as heaven itself?
       O in this love you love your child so ill,
       That you run mad, seeing that she is well.
       She 's not well married that lives married long,
       But she 's best married that dies married young.
       Dry up your tears, and stick your rosemary
       On this fair corse; and as the custom is,   80
       All in her best array bear her to church.
       For though fond nature bids us all lament,
       Yet nature's tears are reason's merriment.

CAPULET   All things that we ordained festival
       Turn from their office to black funeral
       Our instruments to melancholy bells;
       Our wedding cheer to a sad burial feast;
       Our solemn hymns to sullen dirges change;
       Our bridal flowers serve for a buried corse;
       And all things change them to the contrary.   90

F. LAWRENCE Sir, go you in, and madam, go with him;

They all leave, except for the Nurse, who begins to
prepare Juliet's body for burial. The musicians, who
had been hired for the wedding, now arrive. Peter,
the Nurse's servant, asks them to play, to cheer him
up. They refuse and after some talk, they leave.

lour: glower

1 ⟩

1 The Musicians realise that they might as well go away
   again since their services are no longer required.
2 Peter asks them to play to cheer him up, but they
   refuse.
3 Peter threatens, in fun, that he will beat them unless
   they play for him.

2 ⟩

3 ⟩

> And go Sir Paris; every one prepare
> To follow this fair corse unto her grave.
> The heavens do lour upon you for some ill;
> Move them no more by crossing their high will.
> *[They all but the Nurse and Musicians go forth,*
> *casting rosemary on her and shutting the curtains*

1ST MUSICIAN Faith we may put up our pipes and be gone.

NURSE   Honest good fellows, ah put up, put up,
        For well you know this is a pitiful case.   *[Exit*

1ST MUSICIAN Ay by my troth, the case may be amended.

Enter PETER

PETER   Musicians, O musicians, 'Heart's ease, Heart's
        ease'.   100
        O and you will have me live, play 'Heart's ease'.

1ST MUSICIAN Why 'Heart's ease'?

PETER   O musicians, because my heart itself plays 'My
        heart is full'. O play me some merry dump to
        comfort me.

1ST MUSICIAN Not a dump we, 'tis no time to play now.

PETER   You will not then?

1ST MUSICIAN No.

PETER   I will then give it you soundly.

1ST MUSICIAN What will you give us?   110

PETER   No money on my faith, but the gleek. I will give
        you the minstrel.

1ST MUSICIAN Then will I give you the serving-creature.

PETER   Then will I lay the serving-creature's dagger on
        your pate. I will carry no crotchets. I'll *re* you, I'll
        fa you. Do you note me?

1ST MUSICIAN An you *re* us and *fa* us, you note us.

2ND MUSICIAN Pray you put up your dagger, and put out your
        wit.

PETER   Then have at you with my wit. I will dry-beat   120
        you with an iron wit, and put up my iron dagger.

Peter sets the musicians a riddle.

4

4 Then he sets them a riddle, which they try to answer but cannot.

5 Peter tells them the answer to the riddle and they all go.

5

Answer me like men.
'When griping grief the heart doth wound,
And doleful dumps the mind oppress,
Then music with her silver sound'–
Why 'silver sound'? Why 'music with her silver
      sound'?
What say you Simon Catling?

1ST MUSICIAN Marry sir, because silver hath a sweet sound.

PETER   Prates. What say you Hugh Rebeck?

2ND MUSICIAN I say 'silver sound', because musicians sound for
          silver.   130

PETER   Prates too. What say you James Soundpost?

3RD MUSICIAN Faith I know not what to say.

PETER   O I cry you mercy; you are the singer. I will say
          for you. It is 'music with her silver sound',
          because such fellows as you have seldom gold for
          sounding.
          'Then music with her silver sound,
          With speedy help doth lend redress.'   [*Exit*

1ST MUSICIAN What a pestilent knave is this same!

2ND MUSICIAN Hang him, Jack! Come we'll in here, tarry   140
          for the mourners, and stay dinner.   [*Exeunt*

ACTIVITIES

Keeping track

Scene 1

1 How long after the previous scene does this one take place?
2 Why has Paris gone to visit Friar Lawrence?
3 When Juliet is alone with the Friar, what does she threaten to do and why?
4 What does he suggest as a way out of her problems?

Scene 3

5 What fears does Juliet express in her long soliloquy?

Scene 4

6 Apart from what has been shown on stage, what has happened between the end of scene 2 and the beginning of this scene?
7 What are the main preparations they are making for the wedding?

Scene 5

8 When the audience at a play knows something that the characters on stage do not know, the effect is called 'dramatic irony'. The same is true if one of the characters on stage knows something that the others do not. (This idea is explained in the Glossary, page 286.) In what ways is this scene an example of dramatic irony and how does it affect the way in which we respond to what the characters do and say?
9 Why do you think Shakespeare included the short scene with Peter and the musicians?

Discussion

1 In scene 1, Juliet goes to Friar Lawrence and threatens to kill herself, as Romeo has threatened earlier (Act 3 scene 3 lines 103-8). Compare the reasons each has to make this threat and the ways in which Friar Lawrence responds.

2 Do you think that Juliet's parents are too easily taken in by her 'conversion' (scene 2)? Why do you think they accept her story so easily?

3 What is the point of scene 4? Think about:
   ● the sequence of action
   ● the need to contrast moods and show variety.

4 Think about the staging of scene 5. In particular consider these points:
   ● the fact that it clearly continues straight on from scene 4 without a break
   ● where Juliet's bed (and bedroom) are
   ● what the Nurse is doing at each stage in lines 1-16
   ● the movements and actions of Lady Capulet and her husband in lines 17-32.

5 The Nurse, Capulet and his wife, and Paris express their grief at Juliet's death in a way that is clearly exaggerated and even somewhat comic. Why did Shakespeare do this?

Character

1 Think about the behaviour of Friar Lawrence in this act. It is possible both to support his actions and also to criticise them. Make lists of the arguments in favour of what he does and against. Then decide for yourself what you think of him.

2 Write up your Character logs for Friar Lawrence and the other characters in Act 4.

Close study

1 Look carefully at Juliet's soliloquy in Act 4 scene 3 lines 14-59.

2 The main part of this speech is devoted to Juliet's vision of what might go wrong after she has taken the Friar's drug. She imagines five different scenarios. Four of them are introduced by a phrase containing the word 'if' and the other begins with the words, 'is it not like that.' Find the five and write down the line numbers of each.

3 For each one write a short sentence describing briefly in your own words what it is that Juliet is afraid of.

4 Pick out one or two images from the speech that you find vivid or striking and describe the picture they conjure up in your mind.

5 If you were Juliet, which of the five would you find most worrying and why?

Writing

Choose one of these topics for writing.

1 Since Capulet's storming row with Juliet in Act 3 scene 5, his behaviour has seemed quite strange to the servants in his house. Two of them talk about what he has been doing and what the reasons for it might be. Write their conversation.

2 The Nurse, Capulet, Lady Capulet, and Paris all attend Juliet's funeral. Choose two of them and write their thoughts as the service proceeds.

Quiz

'Wise' sayings

Who says, and to whom:
1 What must be shall be.
2 'Tis an ill cook that cannot lick his own fingers.
3 Life, living, all is death's.
4 She's best married that dies married young.

What are:
5 a bier?
6 aqua vitae?
7 rosemary?
8 dirges?

Who:
9 calls whom a slug-abed?
10 talks about 'womanish fear'?

In Mantua Romeo has dreamed that he was dead and that Juliet has brought him back to life with a kiss. Balthasar arrives from Verona with the news of Juliet's death. Romeo tells him to prepare for him to send a letter.

the flattering ... sleep: when we sleep we sometimes have dreams which we believe because we *want* to believe them (since they flatter us).

presage: foretell

bosom's lord: heart

leave: permission

how sweet ... joy: when dreams about love can make me so happy, how sweet my real love must be.

Capel's monument: the Capulets' vault

her immortal part: her soul

did leave ... office: gave me that job to do

I defy you, stars: The stars (which in astrology determine our futures) have ordained that Juliet shall die and so be taken away from Romeo. He is determined not to give in to this.

post-horses: horses used to carry mail rapidly from one place to another

Act five

A street in Mantua
Enter ROMEO

ROMEO If I may trust the flattering truth of sleep,
My dreams presage some joyful news at hand.
My bosom's lord sits lightly in his throne;
And all this day an unaccustomed spirit
Lifts me above the ground with cheerful thoughts.
I dreamt my lady came and found me dead–
Strange dream that gives a dead man leave to think–
And breathed such life with kisses in my lips,
That I revived, and was an emperor.
Ah me, how sweet is love itself possessed,   10
When but love's shadows are so rich in joy.

Enter BALTHASAR *his man, booted*

News from Verona. How now Balthasar,
Dost thou not bring me letters from the friar?
How doth my lady? Is my father well?
How doth my Juliet? That I ask again,
For nothing can be ill if she be well.

BALTHASAR Then she is well and nothing can be ill.
Her body sleeps in Capels' monument,
And her immortal part with angels lives.
I saw her laid low in her kindred's vault,   20
And presently took post to tell it you.
O pardon me for bringing these ill news,
Since you did leave it for my office sir.

ROMEO Is it even so? Then I defy you, stars.
Thou knowest my lodging, get me ink and paper,
And hire post-horses; I will hence tonight.

After telling Romeo that there is no message from Friar Lawrence, Balthasar leaves. Romeo speaks alone. He has decided to kill himself. He knows an apothecary (a chemist) who is very poor and can therefore be persuaded to sell him some poison, although this is illegal.

import: foretell

Let's see for means: Now, how can I do it?

apothecary: a chemist, a person who prepared medicines and other drugs

weeds: clothes

overwhelming brows: overhanging eyebrows

Culling of simples: collecting medicinal herbs

meagre: thin

needy: it was the shop of a poor man

account: collection

earthen: earthenware, terracotta

bladders: liquid containers

packthread: thread

cakes of roses: rose petals compressed into cakes for use as perfume

penury: poverty

present death: summary execution - if you were caught selling it you were immediately put to death.

caitiff: miserable

forerun: come before

BALTHASAR I do beseech you sir, have patience.
Your looks are pale and wild, and do import
Some misadventure.

ROMEO   Tush, thou art deceived.
Leave me, and do the thing I bid thee do.   30
Hast thou no letters to me from the friar?

BALTHASAR No my good lord.

ROMEO   No matter. Get thee gone,
And hire those horses; I'll be with thee straight.
                              [*Exit Balthasar*

Well, Juliet, I will lie with thee tonight.
Let's see for means. O mischief thou art swift
To enter in the thought of desperate men.
I do remember an apothecary–
And hereabouts 'a dwells–which late I noted,
In tattered weeds, with overwhelming brows
Culling of simples; meagre were his looks,   40
Sharp misery had worn him to the bones;
And in his needy shop a tortoise hung,
An alligator stuffed, and other skins
Of ill-shaped fishes, and about his shelves
A beggarly account of empty boxes,
Green earthen pots, bladders, and musty seeds,
Remnants of packthread, and old cakes of roses,
Were thinly scattered, to make up a show.
Noting this penury, to myself I said,
'An if a man did need a poison now,   50
Whose sale is present death in Mantua,
Here lives a caitiff wretch would sell it him'.
O this same thought did but forerun my need,
And this same needy man must sell it me.
As I remember, this should be the house.
Being holy day, the beggar's shop is shut.
What ho, apothecary!

Enter APOTHECARY

He finds the apothecary and persuades him to sell the poison. The apothecary tells him that the poison he has sold him is strong enough to kill twenty men. Romeo accepts the poison and goes.

ducat: a gold coin. Romeo is offering him a lot of money.
soon-speeding gear: rapidly acting substance
trunk: body
womb: interior
utters: sells
starveth in thy eyes: show in your starving face
dispatch you straight: kill you immediately
in flesh: in a healthy condition
cordial: medicine or other drink taken to make a person better

APOTHECARY	Who calls so loud?
ROMEO	Come hither man. I see that thou art poor.

ROMEO

Come hither man. I see that thou art poor.
Hold, there is forty ducats, let me have
A dram of poison, such soon-speeding gear   60
As will disperse itself through all the veins,
That the life-weary taker may fall dead,
And that the trunk may be discharged of breath,
As violently as hasty powder fired
Doth hurry from the fatal cannon's womb.

APOTHECARY

Such mortal drugs I have, but Mantua's law
Is death to any he that utters them.

ROMEO

Art thou so bare and full of wretchedness,
And fearest to die? Famine is in thy cheeks,
Need and oppression starveth in thy eyes,   70
Contempt and beggary hangs upon thy back.
The world is not thy friend, nor the world's law,
The world affords no law to make thee rich;
Then be not poor, but break it, and take this.

APOTHECARY

My poverty, but not my will consents.

ROMEO

I pay thy poverty and not thy will.

APOTHECARY

Put this in any liquid thing you will
And drink it off, and if you had the strength
Of twenty men, it would dispatch you straight.

ROMEO

There is thy gold, worse poison to men's souls,   80
Doing more murder in this loathsome world,
Than these poor compounds that thou mayst
    not sell.
I sell thee poison, thou hast sold me none.
Farewell, buy food, and get thyself in flesh.
Come cordial, and not poison, go with me
To Juliet's grave, for there must I use thee.

[*Exeunt*

In Verona Friar Lawrence is visited by Friar John from Mantua. John tells him that there has been an outbreak of plague in Mantua and so he has been unable to deliver Friar Lawrence's letter to Romeo. Lawrence prepares to go to the Capulets' tomb immediately to rescue Juliet.

1 Friar John arrives from Mantua and greets Friar Lawrence, who asks him about Romeo's reply to his letter.

2 Friar John explains that he has not delivered it. His companion had been found visiting the sick by local health officials. They thought the two friars might have been in contact with the plague and so locked them in their own house (in quarantine).

3 He shows Friar Lawrence the letter, which he has been unable to give to Romeo.

4 Dismayed at this news, Friar Lawrence sends John to get tools with which he can break into the Capulets' vault.

5 He tells us that Juliet will awaken in three hours' time and he must be there. He will hide her at his cell until he can arrange for Romeo to come to her.

1 ⟩

2 ⟩

3 ⟩

4 ⟩

5 ⟩

SCENE 2

Friar Lawrence's cell
Enter FRIAR JOHN

F. JOHN Holy Franciscan friar, brother, ho!

Enter FRIAR LAWRENCE

F. LAWRENCE This same should be the voice of Friar John.
Welcome from Mantua. What says Romeo?
Or if his mind be writ, give me his letter.

F. JOHN Going to find a bare-foot brother out,
One of our order, to associate me,
Here in this city visiting the sick,
And finding him, the searchers of the town,
Suspecting that we both were in a house
Where the infectious pestilence did reign,   10
Sealed up the doors, and would not let us forth,
So that my speed to Mantua there was stayed.

F. LAWRENCE Who bare my letter then to Romeo?

F. JOHN I could not send it, here it is again—
Nor get a messenger to bring it thee,
So fearful were they of infection.

F. LAWRENCE Unhappy fortune! By my brotherhood,
The letter was not nice, but full of charge
Of dear import; and the neglecting it
May do much danger. Friar John, go hence,   20
Get me an iron crow and bring it straight
Unto my cell.

F. JOHN   Brother I'll go and bring it thee. [*Exit*

F. LAWRENCE Now must I to the monument alone;
Within this three hours will fair Juliet wake.
She will beshrew me much that Romeo
Hath had no notice of these accidents.

Paris arrives at Juliet's tomb accompanied by his
Page. Sending the Page to keep watch he lays flowers
on the grave and speaks of his grief at Juliet's death.
The Page warns him that someone is coming and he
hides.

aloof: some distance away
all along: flat on the ground
sweet water: perfumed water
obsequies: memorial ceremony
cross: interrupt
rite: ceremony
Muffle: hide

But I will write again to Mantua,
And keep her at my cell till Romeo come—
Poor living corse closed in a dead man's tomb.

[Exit

SCENE **3**

A churchyard, outside the tomb of the Capulets
Enter PARIS *and his Page with flowers and sweet water*

PARIS
Give me thy torch boy. Hence, and stand aloof.
Yet put it out, for I would not be seen.
Under yond yew trees lay thee all along,
Holding thy ear close to the hollow ground;
So shall no foot upon the churchyard tread,
Being loose, unfirm, with digging up of graves,
But thou shalt hear it; whistle then to me,
As signal that thou hearest something approach.
Give me those flowers. Do as I bid thee, go.

PAGE
I am almost afraid to stand alone   10
Here in the churchyard, yet I will adventure.

[Paris strews the tomb with flowers

PARIS
Sweet flower, with flowers thy bridal bed I strew.
O woe, thy canopy is dust and stones,
Which with sweet water nightly I will dew,
Or wanting that, with tears distilled by moans.
The obsequies that I for thee will keep,
Nightly shall be to strew thy grave and weep.

[Page whistles

The boy gives warning something doth approach.
What cursed foot wanders this way tonight,
To cross my obsequies and true love's rite?   20
What, with a torch? Muffle me night awhile.

[Retires

**It is Romeo, with his servant Balthasar. Romeo takes
the tools Balthasar is carrying and, after giving him a
letter for his father, tells him to go. Balthasar says he
will, but only goes just out of sight because he is
worried about what Romeo will do. Romeo starts to
open Juliet's tomb, but Paris comes out of his hiding
place and tries to stop him.**

mattock: pickaxe
wrenching iron: crowbar
But chiefly … ring: Romeo gives this as his excuse for
    wanting to open Juliet's tomb.
in dear employment: for a purpose that is very important
    to me
jealous: suspicious
inexorable: relentless
empty: hungry
For all this same: in spite of what he says
his intents I doubt: I am worried about what he is
    planning to do.
maw: stomach

Enter ROMEO *and* BALTHASAR *with a torch, a
mattock, and a crow of iron*

ROMEO Give me that mattock and the wrenching-iron.
Hold, take this letter. Early in the morning
See thou deliver it to my lord and father.
Give me the light. Upon thy life I charge thee,
Whate'er thou hearest or seest, stand all aloof,
And do not interrupt me in my course.
Why I descend into this bed of death,
Is partly to behold my lady's face;
But chiefly to take thence from her dead finger   30
A precious ring, a ring that I must use
In dear employment. Therefore hence, be gone.
But if thou, jealous, dost return to pry
In what I farther shall intend to do,
By heaven I will tear thee joint by joint,
And strew this hungry churchyard with thy limbs.
The time and my intents are savage-wild,
More fierce and more inexorable far
Than empty tigers, or the roaring sea.

BALTHASAR I will be gone sir, and not trouble you.   40

ROMEO So shalt thou show me friendship. Take thou that.
Live and be prosperous, and farewell good fellow.

BALTHASAR [*Aside*] For all this same, I'll hide me hereabout.
His looks I fear, and his intents I doubt.   [*Retires*

ROMEO Thou destestable maw, thou womb of death,
Gorged with the dearest morsel of the earth,
Thus I enforce thy rotten jaws to open,
                                        [*Opens the tomb*
And in despite I'll cram thee with more food.

PARIS This is that banished haughty Montague,
That murdered my love's cousin, with which
    grief   50
It is supposed the fair creature died,

Romeo tells him that he is desperate and that Paris should not tempt his anger, but Paris persists. They fight and Paris is killed. It is only then that Romeo realises who he has killed and why he was there. He proceeds to open the tomb and, as Paris had requested before he died, places the body of Paris beside Juliet.

unhallowed toil: unholy work
apprehend: arrest
conjuration: appeal
felon: criminal
peruse: look at
betossed: disturbed
One writ ... book: he sees Paris as someone like himself, destined to be unfortunate

And here is come to do some villainous shame
To the dead bodies. I will apprehend him.
Stop thy unhallowed toil, vile Montague.
Can vengeance be pursued further than death?
Condemned villain, I do apprehend thee.
Obey and go with me, for thou must die.

ROMEO I must indeed, and therefore came I hither.
Good gentle youth, tempt not a desperate man;
Fly hence and leave me; think upon these
            gone;   60
Let them affright thee. I beseech thee youth,
Put not another sin upon my head,
By urging me to fury. O be gone.
By heaven, I love thee better than myself,
For I come hither armed against myself.
Stay not, be gone, live, and hereafter say,
A madman's mercy bid thee run away.

PARIS I do defy thy conjuration,
And apprehend thee for a felon here.

ROMEO Wilt thou provoke me? Then have at thee boy.   70
                                            [*They fight*

PAGE O Lord, they fight! I will go call the watch.   [*Exit*

PARIS O I am slain. If thou be merciful,
Open the tomb, lay me with Juliet.

ROMEO In faith I will. Let me peruse this face.
Mercutio's kinsman, noble County Paris!
What said my man, when my betossed soul
Did not attend him as we rode? I think
He told me Paris should have married Juliet.
Said he not so? Or did I dream it so?
Or am I mad, hearing him talk of Juliet,   80
To think it was so? O give me thy hand,
One writ with me in sour misfortune's book.
I'll bury thee in a triumphant grave.
A grave? O no, a lantern, slaughtered youth;
For here lies Juliet, and her beauty makes

Romeo is struck by Juliet's beauty. Swearing that he will stay with her forever, he swallows the poison and dies.

by a dead man interred: literally, buried by a dead man. Romeo is going to kill himself and sees himself as already dead.

lightning: lightening

ensign: flag carried in battle. Romeo is talking about the battle between life and death for possession of Juliet's body.

unsubstantial death is amorous: bodiless death is in love (with Juliet)

abhorred: that we shrink from in horror

paramour: lover

shake the ... stars: shake off the burden imposed by fate

seal with ... death: make an eternal bargain with death that wants to take possession of our lives and seal with a kiss

Come bitter ... bark: Romeo compares his willpower to the pilot and his body to the boat which is being steered onto the rocks of death.

This vault a feasting presence full of light.
Death, lie thou there, by a dead man interred.

[*Lays Paris in the monument*

How oft when men are at the point of death
Have they been merry, which their keepers call
A lightning before death. O how may I   90
Call this a lightning? O my love, my wife!
Death that hath sucked the honey of thy breath
Hath had no power yet upon thy beauty.
Thou art not conquered; beauty's ensign yet
Is crimson in thy lips and in thy cheeks,
And death's pale flag is not advanced there.
Tybalt, liest thou there in thy bloody sheet?
O what more favour can I do to thee,
Than with that hand that cut thy youth in twain
To sunder his that was thine enemy?   100
Forgive me cousin. Ah dear Juliet,
Why art thou yet so fair? Shall I believe
That unsubstantial death is amorous,
And that the lean abhorred monster keeps
Thee here in dark to be his paramour?
For fear of that, I still will stay with thee,
And never from this palace of dim night
Depart again. Here, here will I remain
With worms that are thy chamber-maids. O here
Will I set up my everlasting rest;   110
And shake the yoke of inauspicious stars
From this world-wearied flesh. Eyes look your last.
Arms, take your last embrance. And lips, O you
The doors of breath, seal with a righteous kiss
A dateless bargain to engrossing death.
[*Takes out the poison*] Come bitter conduct, come
    unsavoury guide.
Thou desperate pilot, now at once run on
The dashing rocks thy sea-sick weary bark.
Here's to my love! [*drinks*] O true apothecary!
Thy drugs are quick. Thus with a kiss I die.   120

Nearby, Friar Lawrence, hurrying towards the tomb, meets Balthasar, who tells him that Romeo is already there. The Friar finds the bodies of Romeo and Paris.

As I discern: As far as I can see

his intents: what he was planning to do

some ill unthrifty thing: some evil unlucky thing

sepulchre: burial place

masterless: They have been thrown down and so have no 'masters'.

Ah what...chance: What unnatural moment led to this sorrowful event.

Enter FRIAR LAWRENCE, *with lantern, crow and spade*

F. LAWRENCE Saint Francis be my speed. How oft tonight
Have my old feet stumbled at graves. Who's there?

BALTHASAR Here's one, a friend, and one that knows you well.

F. LAWRENCE Bliss be upon you. Tell me, good my friend.
What torch is yond, that vainly lends his light
To grubs and eyeless skulls? As I discern,
It burneth in the Capels' monument.

BALTHASAR It doth so holy sir, and there's my master,
One that you love.

F. LAWRENCE   Who is it?

BALTHASAR   Romeo.   129

F. LAWRENCE How long hath he been there?

BALTHASAR   Full half an hour.

F. LAWRENCE Go with me to the vault.

BALTHASAR   I dare not sir.
My master knows not but I am gone hence;
And fearfully did menace me with death,
If I did stay to look on his intents.

F. LAWRENCE Stay then, I'll go alone. Fear comes upon me.
O much I fear some ill unthrifty thing.

BALTHASAR As I did sleep under this yew tree here,
I dreamt my master and another fought,
And that my master slew him.

F. LAWRENCE   Romeo!
                    [*Stoops and looks on the blood and weapons*
Alack, alack, what blood is this which stains   140
The stony entrance of this sepulchre?
What mean these masterless and gory swords
To lie discoloured by this place of peace?
                                   [*Enters the monument*
Romeo! O pale! Who else! What, Paris too?
And steeped in blood? Ah what an unkind hour
Is guilty of this lamentable chance!

At this moment Juliet begins to wake up. Friar
Lawrence tells her what has happened and tries to
hurry her away because he has heard a noise but
Juliet refuses to leave. Afraid of what may happen, he
goes. Juliet sees that Romeo has poisoned himself.
Hearing people coming she takes Romeo's dagger and
kills herself. Led by Paris's Page, the Watchmen
discover the bodies of Romeo, Juliet and Paris.

contagion: poisonous influences
sisterhood of holy nuns: a nunnery
hath been ... end: has killed him
churl: ill-mannered person (but Juliet is saying it
    affectionately)
restorative: she kisses him (which in fairy tales would
    restore him to life)

The lady stirs.   [*Juliet rises*

JULIET   O comfortable friar, where is my lord?
                I do remember well where I should be,
                And there I am. Where I my Romeo?   150
                                                  [*Noise within*

F. LAWRENCE   I hear some noise. Lady, come from that nest
                Of death, contagion, and unnatural sleep.
                A greater power than we can contradict
                Hath thwarted our intents. Come, come away.
                Thy husband in thy bosom there lies dead;
                And Paris too. Come I'll dispose of thee
                Among a sisterhood of holy nuns.
                Stay not to question, for the watch is coming.
                Come, go good Juliet, I dare no longer stay.
                                            [*Exit Friar Lawrence*

JULIET   Go get thee hence, for I will not away.   160
                What's here? A cup closed in my true love's hand?
                Poison I see hath been his timeless end.
                O churl, drunk all, and left no friendly drop
                To help me after? I will kiss thy lips;
                Haply some poison yet doth hang on them,
                To make me die with a restorative.
                Thy lips are warm.

FIRST WATCH [*Within*]   Lead, boy. Which way?

JULIET   Yea, noise? Then I'll be brief. O happy dagger!
                                          [*Draws Romeo's dagger*
                This is thy sheath; there rest, and let me die.
                                              [*She stabs herself*

                Enter Watch, with the Page of PARIS

PAGE   This is the place; there where the torch doth
                  burn.   170

FIRST WATCH   The ground is bloody, search about the churchyard.
                Go some of you, whoe'er you find attach.
                                        [*Exeunt some of the Watch*
                Pitiful sight! Here lies the County slain,

**Another Watchman has arrested Friar Lawrence and
brings him back to the tomb. They are followed by the
Prince and the Capulets, who express their horror at
the sight before them.**

We see ... descry: a play on words. 'ground' means (a) the
place where the bodies are (b) the reason why they are
there
descry: make out
misadventure: unfortunate event

And Juliet bleeding, warm, and newly dead,
Who here hath lain this two days buried.
Go tell the Prince, run to the Capulets,
Raise up the Montagues, some others search.

[Exeunt others of the Watch

We see the ground whereon these woes do lie,
But the true ground of all these piteous woes
We cannot without circumstance descry.   180

Enter some of the Watch with BALTHASAR

2ND WATCH Here's Romeo's man, we found him in the
churchyard.

1ST WATCH Hold him in safety, till the Prince come hither.

Enter FRIAR LAWRENCE *with another Watchman*

3RD WATCH Here is a friar that trembles, sighs, and weeps.
We took this mattock and this spade from him,
As he was coming from this churchyard's side.

1ST WATCH A great suspicion. Stay the friar too.

Enter the PRINCE *and Attendants*

PRINCE What misadventure is so early up.
That calls our person from our morning rest?

Enter CAPULET *and* LADY CAPULET

CAPULET What should it be that is so shriekt abroad?

L. CAPULET The people in the street cry 'Romeo';   190
Some 'Juliet', and some 'Paris', and all run
With open outcry toward our monument.

PRINCE What fear is this which startles in your ears?

1ST WATCH Sovereign, here lies the County Paris slain,
And Romeo dead, and Juliet, dead before,
Warm and new killed.

PRINCE Search, seek, and know how this foul murder
comes.

**Montague arrives on the scene, explains that his wife
has died and expresses his grief at his son's death. At
the Prince's command, Friar Lawrence begins to
explain the sequence of events that has led to the
tragedy.**

lo, his...bosom: The scabbard Romeo wore is empty and the
dagger has wrongly been 'sheathed' in Juliet's body.
untaught: Romeo has not learned his manners and has
pushed in front of his father to die before him.

1 The Prince tells them to calm their grief for a while until
they know what has happened.
2 The Friar offers to tell them all.

1ST WATCH	Here is a friar, and slaughtered Romeo's man,
	With instruments upon them, fit to open
	These dead men's tombs. 200
CAPULET	O heavens! O wife, look how our daughter bleeds.
	This dagger hath mista'en, for lo his house
	Is empty on the back of Montague,
	And is mis-sheathed in my daughter's bosom.
L. CAPULET	O me, this sight of death is as a bell,
	That warns my old age to a sepulchre.

Enter MONTAGUE

PRINCE	Come Montague, for thou art early up,
	To see thy son and heir more early down.
MONTAGUE	Alas my liege, my wife is dead tonight.
	Grief of my son's exile hath stopped her breath. 210
	What further woe conspires against mine age?
PRINCE	Look and thou shalt see.
MONTAGUE	O thou untaught, what manners is in this,
	To press before thy father to a grave?
PRINCE	Seal up the mouth of outrage for a while,
	Till we can clear these ambiguities,
	And know their spring, their head, their true
	descent;
	And then will I be general of your woes,
	And lead you even to death. Meantime forbear,
	And let mischance be slave to patience. 220
	Bring forth the parties of suspicion.
F. LAWRENCE	I am the greatest, able to do least,
	Yet most suspected, as the time and place
	Doth make against me, of this direful murder.
	And here I stand both to impeach and purge
	Myself condemned, and myself excused.
PRINCE	Then say at once what thou dost know in this.
F. LAWRENCE	I will be brief, for my short date of breath
	Is not so long as is a tedious tale.
	Romeo, there dead, was husband to that Juliet; 230

**Friar Lawrence explains the sequence of events that
has led to the tragedy.**

3 He then outlines the events that led to the three
deaths. Romeo and Juliet were married by him on the
day that Tybalt died and it was Romeo's banishment
that caused Juliet so much unhappiness.

4 Capulet then arranged for her to marry Paris and she
asked the Friar to help her.

5 He gave her a drug to make it look as if she was dead
and wrote to Romeo telling him what had happened
and what to do.

6 Unfortunately the letter was never delivered, so he
went to Juliet's tomb to take her away when she
awoke.

7 When he got there he found Romeo and Paris dead.
When Juliet awoke he tried, unsuccessfully, to
persuade her to come away. Apparently she killed
herself.

8 The Friar says that if he is at fault he is willing to die.

And she, there dead, that Romeo's faithful wife.
I married them, and their stolen marriage-day
Was Tybalt's dooms-day, whose untimely death
Banished the new-made bridegroom from this city;
For whom, and not for Tybalt, Juliet pined.
You, to remove that siege of grief from her,
Betrothed, and would have married her perforce,
To County Paris. Then comes she to me,
And, with wild looks, bid me devise some mean
To rid her from this second marriage,   240
Or in my cell there would she kill herself.
Then gave I her, so tutored by my art,
A sleeping potion, which so took effect
As I intended, for it wrought on her
The form of death. Meantime I writ to Romeo,
That he should hither come as this dire night,
To help to take her from her borrowed grave,
Being the time the potion's force should cease.
But he which bore my letter, Friar John,
Was stayed by accident, and yesternight   250
Returned my letter back. Then all alone
At the prefixed hour of her waking,
Came I to take her from her kindred's vault,
Meaning to keep her closely at my cell,
Till I conveniently could send to Romeo.
But when I came, some minute ere the time
Of her awakening, here untimely lay
The noble Paris and true Romeo dead.
She wakes, and I entreated her come forth,
And bear this work of heaven with patience.   260
But then a noise did scare me from the tomb,
And she, too desperate, would not go with me,
But, as it seems, did violence on herself.
All this I know, and to the marriage
Her Nurse is privy; and if aught in this
Miscarried by my fault, let my old life

Further details are supplied by Balthaser, who gives the Prince Romeo's letter, and by Paris's Page. The Prince reads the letter which confirms the Friar's story. Capulet and Montague realise that it is their feud which has led to the tragedy and they agree to abandon all hostility. They will raise statues of Romeo and Juliet as a memorial to their children and to show that the two families are now at peace.

9 The Prince then turns to Balthasar who tells him how he took news of Juliet's death to Romeo and accompanied him to the tomb. He has a letter Romeo gave him.

10 The Prince takes the letter and asks Paris's Page what he can tell them. The Page explains why Paris came to the grave and how he fought with Romeo.

tidings: news
pothecary: apothecary
therewithal: with it
scourge: punishment
laid upon: caused by
winking at: turning a blind eye to
a brace of kinsmen: Paris and Mercutio were both relatives of the Prince
jointure: marriage settlement, money and goods given by the groom's family to the bride at the time of the wedding
whiles: as long as
There shall ... set: No statue shall ever be as highly valued

Be sacrificed some hour before his time,
Unto the rigour of severest law.

PRINCE We still have known thee for a holy man.
Where's Romeo's man? What can he say in
this?   270

BALTHASAR I brought my master news of Juliet's death,
And then in post he came from Mantua
To this same place, to this same monument.
This letter he early bid me give his father,
And threatened me with death, going in the vault,
If I departed not, and left him there.

PRINCE Give me the letter, I will look on it.
Where is the County's page, that raised the Watch?
Sirrah, what made your master in this place?

PAGE He came with flowers to strew his lady's grave,   280
And bid me stand aloof, and so I did.
Anon comes one with light to ope the tomb,
And by and by my master drew on him,
And then I ran away to call the Watch.

PRINCE This letter doth make good the friar's words,
Their course of love, the tidings of her death.
And here he writes that he did buy a poison
Of a poor pothecary, and therewithal
Came to this vault to die and lie with Juliet.
Where be these enemies? Capulet, Montague,   290
See what a scourge is laid upon your hate,
That heaven finds means to kill your joys with love.
And I for winking at your discords too
Have lost a brace of kinsmen; all are punished.

CAPULET O brother Montague, give me thy hand.
This is my daughter's jointure, for no more
Can I demand.

MONTAGUE   But I can give thee more.
For I will raise her statue in pure gold,
That whiles Verona by that name is known,
There shall no figure at such rate be set   300

glooming: dark

Keeping track

Scene 1

1 When and where does this scene take place?
2 What is Romeo's mood at the beginning of the scene?
3 What picture do you get of the apothecary and his shop?
4 Why does the apothecary agree to sell Romeo the forbidden poison?

Scene 2

5 When and where does this scene take place?
6 Where does Friar Lawrence have to hurry and why?

As that of true and faithful Juliet.

CAPULET As rich shall Romeo by his lady lie,
Poor sacrifices of our enmity.

PRINCE A glooming peace this morning with it brings;
The sun for sorrow will not show his head.
Go hence to have more talk of these sad things;
Some shall be pardoned, and some punished.
For never was a story of more woe
Than this of Juliet and her Romeo [*Exeunt*

Scene 3

7 When and where does this scene take place?
8 Why does Paris go to Juliet's tomb?
9 What excuse does Romeo give to Balthasar for wanting to open Juliet's tomb? Why?
10 Why does Romeo kill Paris?
11 Why does Friar Lawrence leave Juliet on her own?
12 What do Montague and Capulet agree to do at the end of the play?

Discussion

1 What is your opinion of the apothecary and his behaviour?
2 What is the point of scene 2 - is it necessary for the plot of the play?
3 Scene 3 is quite long and fairly complicated. Divide it into a number of main sections and give each one a short title that sums up the action in that part of the scene.

Drama

'Poor sacrifices of our enmity'

Groups of four or five.
After the tragedy Montague and Capulet agree to erect golden statues to their children.

1 Imagine you are the sculptors who have been given this commission (see page 263).
2 Work in groups to produce a selection of statues.
3 Decide as a class which is the most appropriate statue - it may be necessary to select certain details from different statues.
4 Decide on an inscription.

Character

Romeo

On the basis of what happens in this act, you could sum Romeo up as a vicious killer and a suicide who can't face up to reality. Would that be a fair judgment? If not, why not?

Montague and Capulet

What is your judgment of the heads of the two families at the end of the play:

• Have they learned anything from the deaths of their children?
• How much blame attaches to them for the deaths of their children?

Close study

In the early part of scene 3 both Paris and Romeo speak over Juliet's grave and try to express their feelings about her (lines 12-17 and 91-6). Make a comparison of these two speeches. Think about these questions:
- What aspect of Juliet and her death does each focus on?
- What images does each use?
- Which has the more powerful effect on you as a reader and why?

Writing

1 At the beginning of Scene 3 (line 23) we learn that Romeo has written a letter to his father explaining what has happened - to be read after his death. Write what you think must have been in the letter. (If you read the whole scene carefully, you will find some helpful clues later on.)
2 Write either obituaries (prose) or epitaphs (verse) for Romeo and Juliet.
3 Friar Lawrence
  In Act 5 everything that Friar Lawrence has tried to do falls apart. Make notes on these topics:
  - What he tries to do.
  - How it goes wrong.
  - Why it goes wrong.
  - How his behaviour in this act changes your assessment of his character (if it does).

  Now write a balanced judgment of his character.

Explorations

Keeping track

When you are studying a play one of the most difficult things to do is to keep track of all the ideas and information you gain as you work on it scene by scene. It is important to keep a note of what you do. Two good ways of organising your work are to keep a Scene log and a Character log.

Scene log

As you work on each scene, make a list of the basic information about it:
- when and where it takes place
- the characters in it
- what happens.

Then add any thoughts and comments you want to remember. You could use the layout illustrated opposite - or you may prefer to make up your own.

Character log

At the same time, you can keep a log for each of the main characters. Use this to record what you find out about the character in every scene he or she appears in:
- key points about the character
- your reasons for choosing these points
- the numbers of important lines
- short quotations to back up the key points.

Again, there is a layout opposite, but you may prefer to develop your own approach.

Scene Log

Act/scene	Time/Place	Characters	Action	Comments
1/2	Sunday afternoon, Capulet's house	Capulet, Paris	Paris asks Capulet if he can marry Juliet. Capulet says she's too young, but he will ask her. He invites Paris to the feast.	Capulet seems very considerate about his daughter.

Character Log

Character: Capulet			
Act/scene	Key points	Reasons	Key lines	Short quotations
1/2	Thoughtful about Juliet and her age	He wants Paris to wait two years, till she's 16	8–11	
	Juliet is 'the apple of his eye'	She's his only surviving child	13–15	Earth hath swallowed all my hopes but she

Drama activities

Most of these activities can be done in small groups or by the class as a whole. They work by slowing down the action of the play and helping you focus on a small section of it - so that you can think more deeply about characters, plot and themes.

Hotseating

Hotseating means putting one of the characters 'under the microscope' at a particular point in the play. This is how it works:

1 Begin by choosing a particular character and a particular moment in the play. For example you might choose Tybalt at the moment when he provokes Benvolio to draw his sword (Act 1 scene 1).
2 One person (student or teacher) is selected to be the chosen character.
3 That person sits 'in the hot seat', with the rest of the group arranged round in a semi-circle, or a circle.
4 The rest then ask questions about how the character feels, why s/he has acted in that way, and so on. Try to keep the questions going and not to give the person in the hotseat too much time to think.

Variations

1 The questioners themselves take on roles. (In the example above they could be the Prince's men.)
2 Characters can be hotseated at a series of key moments in a scene to see how their opinions and attitudes change.
3 The questioners can take different attitudes to the character. For example:
   ● aggressive
   ● pleading
   ● disbelieving.

Freeze!

It is very useful to be able to 'stop the action' and concentrate on a single moment in the play. You can do this in a number of ways.

Photographs

Imagine that someone has taken a photograph of a particular moment, or that (as if it were a film or video) the action has been frozen. Once you have chosen the moment, you can work in a number of different ways:

- Act that part of the scene and then 'Freeze!' - you will probably find it easier if you have a 'director' standing outside the scene to shout 'Freeze!'
- Discuss what the photograph should look like and then arrange yourselves into the photograph.
- One at a time place yourselves in the photograph; each person 'entering' it must take notice of what is there already.
- Once you have arranged the photograph, take it in turns to come out of it and comment on it, with suggestions for improvements.

There are a number of ways in which you can develop your photograph:

- Each person takes it in turn to speak his/her thoughts at that moment in the scene.
- The photograph is given a caption.
- Some members of the group do not take part in the photograph. Instead they provide a sound track of speech or sound effects, or both.

Statues

Make a statue like this:
1 Select a moment in the play, or a title from the play (eg 'star-cross'd lovers').
2 Choose one member of the group to be the sculptor. That person then arranges the rest of the group, one at

a time to make the statue. Statues are different from photographs in two important ways:

- they are made by a 'sculptor' and tell us about the sculptor's view of the person or event;
- if they talk, they tell us about what they can 'see'. For example if there was a statue of the fight between Tybalt and Mercutio, placed in the streets of Verona, it could only 'tell' us about how the citizens of Verona behaved when they saw it. (If you want Tybalt and Mercutio to speak of their thoughts at that moment, then hotseat them, or make a photograph.)

Forum theatre

In Forum theatre, one or two people take on roles and the rest of the group are 'directors'. It works like this:

1 Select a moment in the play. (For example the moment when Romeo sees Juliet for the first time.)
2 Select a member of the group to be Romeo.
3 Organise your working area, so that everyone knows where the other characters are, where characters make entrances and exits, and so on.
4 Begin by asking Romeo to offer his own first thoughts about position, gesture, and movement.
5 The directors then experiment with different ways of presenting that moment. They can:
   - ask Romeo to take up a particular position, use a particular gesture, move in a certain way;
   - ask him to speak in a particular way;
   - discuss with Romeo how he might move or speak and why - for example to communicate a certain set of thoughts and feelings.
6 The short sequence can be repeated a number of times, until the directors have used up all their ideas about their interpretation.

Shakespeare's language

It is easy to look at the text of this play and say to yourself, 'I'm never going to understand that!' But it is important not to be put off. Remember that there are two reasons why Shakespeare's language may seem strange at first:

1 He was writing four hundred years ago and the English language has changed over the centuries.
2 He wrote mainly in verse. As a result he sometimes changed the order of words to make them fit the verse form, and he used a large number of 'tricks of the trade': figures of speech and other techniques.

On page 268 you will find advice on tackling the 'difficult bits'.

Language change

This can cause three main kinds of problem:

Grammar

Since the end of the 16th century, there have been some changes in English grammar. Some examples:

1 Thee, thou, thy, and the verb forms that go with them:
> O gentle Romeo,
> If *thou dost* love, pronounce it faithfully.
> Or if *thou thinkest* I am too quickly won,
> I'll frown, and be perverse, and say *thee* nay,
> So *thou wilt* woo.

2 Words contract (shorten) in different ways. For example:
   'tis rather than *it's*
   who is't for *who is it*

3 Some of the 'little words' are different. For example:
   an for *if.*

Words that have changed their meaning

Sometimes you will come across words that you think you know, but then discover that they don't mean what you expect them to mean. For example:
presently (Act 4 scene 1 line 54) meant *at once* in Shakespeare's day. Now it means *in a while*.
Nowadays if you are *fond* of someone, you like them quite a lot. But in Act 2 scene 2 line 98, it means *excessively, madly in love*.

Words that have gone out of use

These are the most obvious and most frequent causes of difficulty. Shakespeare had - and used - a huge vocabulary. He loved using words, and pushing them to their limits. So you will come across many words you have not met before. They are usually explained in the notes. But before rushing to look up every single word, remember the advice at the bottom of page 268.

The language of the play

Most of *Romeo & Juliet* is in *blank verse*, but parts are in *prose* and short sections are in *rhymed verse*.

Blank verse

The main part of the play is written in lines of ten syllables, with a repeated even pattern of weak and strong 'beats':
*In fair Verona **where** we **lay** our **scene***
(ti **tum** ti **tum** ti **tum** ti **tum** ti **tum**)
If Shakespeare had made every line exactly the same, the play would soon become very monotonous, so he varies the rhythm in a number of ways. Often he just changes the pattern of weak and strong slightly:
Which, *but their* **children's end naught** *could re***move**
(**tum** ti ti **tum** ti **tum tum** ti ti **tum**)
He also writes so that sentences sometimes end at the

end of a line, and at other times in the middle:

God's bread! It makes me mad.
Day, night; hour, tide, time; work, play;
Alone, in company; still my care hath been
To have her matched.

So the verse of the play has a strong but varied rhythm.
Most of the lines do not rhyme, so they are 'blank' -
hence the term *blank verse*.

Rhymed verse

Sometimes Shakespeare uses a pattern of rhymed lines. It
may be just two successive lines (a *rhyming couplet*):

ROMEO: Farewell. Thou canst not teach me to forget.
BENVOLIO: I'll pay that doctrine, or else die in debt.

Rhyming couplets often round off a scene, but they are
also used in the middles of scenes. Sometimes there is a
more complicated pattern of rhymes:

ROMEO: When the devout religion of mine eye
Maintains such falsehood, then turn tears to
fires;
And these, who, often drowned, could never die,
Transparent heretics, be burnt for liars!
One fairer than my love? The all-seeing sun
Ne'er saw her match since first the world begun.

This pattern is taken from the *sonnet*, a popular form for
love poems. Shakespeare uses this effect sparingly and
usually when characters are talking about love.

Prose

In some scenes, characters' speeches are not written in
blank or rhymed verse, but in 'ordinary sentences' -
prose. If you look at the play as a whole, you will see that
prose is used for certain characters and situations. Look,
for example, at these sections:

Act 1 scene 1 lines 1-61; Act 2 scene 4 (whole scene).
Work out what you think those characters and situations
are.

Working out the difficult bits

If you come across a section of the play that you find
difficult to understand, try any or all of these approaches:

1 Read the whole section through and try to get an idea
   of the gist of it - roughly what it is about.
2 Try to pin down which particular sentences are
   causing the problem.
3 Work out the pattern of the whole sentence - look to
   see if Shakespeare has changed the ordinary word
   order to fit the verse.
4 Try reading the sentence aloud a few times.
5 Don't feel that you have to understand every word in
   the play - very few people do!
6 Don't feel that you've got to read every note and
   explanation in this book - use them when you really
   need them.

Themes

Conflict

Two households, both alike in dignity
  In fair Verona, where we lay our scene,
From ancient grudge break to new mutiny,
  Where civil blood makes civil hands unclean.

Modern day examples

The conflict between the Montagues and the Capulets
seemed to divide and disturb all Verona. Conflicts that
divide whole communities in this way are not uncommon
today.
Work in small groups.
1 Think of as many examples of conflicts within
   communities as you can and list them.
2 Choose one such conflict and discuss its causes and
   effects. List as many of each as you can.
3 Collect evidence about the conflict you have chosen by
   doing some research in newspapers and on radio and
   television news bulletins.
4 Use the material you have collected to make a poster
   illustrating the conflict. Try to present it so that it
   shows:
   ● the intensity of the conflict
   ● its causes
   ● its effects
   ● the opinions of each side.

Montagues and Capulets

Work in small groups.
1 Collect all the evidence you can about the conflict
   between the two families:
   ● what supporters of each side say about the other
     side

- what neutrals say about the conflict
- what happens when the conflict breaks out into actual fighting.
2 Use the material you have collected as the basis for a presentation to the rest of the class:
  - an anthology of quotations with a commentary by you either written out as a booklet or rehearsed and performed
  - a recorded 'radio programme'
  - a poster.

Love

If you ask anyone what *Romeo and Juliet* is 'about', their answer will almost certainly contain the word 'love'. But this is a word that means different things to different characters in the play, and for some, like Romeo, its meaning changes as the play progresses.

Romeo and love

At the beginning of the play, Romeo is presented as a young man desperately in love. It affects his behaviour so badly that his father is concerned about him (Act 1 scene 1 lines 129-140). He is clearly feeling very 'mixed up' (Act 1 scene 1 lines 154-182) and compares being in love to being mad or in prison (Act 1 scene 2 lines 55-57). This is because he loves a young woman, Rosaline, who does not return his love. He has tried all the conventional approaches (Act 1 scene 1 lines 206-214) and all have failed. Despite this, his love is like a religion (Act 1 scene 2 lines 90-95) and anyone who denies it is a 'heretic' or false believer.

Fashionable young men and women of the time considered that such thoughts and feelings were suitable for true 'love': the young man fell in love with a beautiful young woman, often with little hope of winning her love in return. All he could do was worship from a distance and hope for occasional small favours - a smile in his direction, for

example. Such love did not normally lead to marriage. That
was something different and was arranged between families; it
concerned legal contracts, family pride, money. Love either
did not enter into it at all, or only as a secondary
consideration, as it does in the conversation between Paris
and Capulet (Act 1 scene 2 lines 7-19).

Research

1 Look up the quotations listed so far. Make sure that you
   understand them and the attitude to love they describe.
2 Now look up the following quotations and see how
   Romeo's attitude changes:
   Act 1 scene 5 lines 43-52 (especially compare lines 51-
   52 with Act 1 scene 2 lines 90-95) and lines 92-109.
3 Now work through the play and find quotations that
   show how Romeo's view of love changes through his
   relationship with Juliet. Some key scenes to look at are:
   Act 2 scene 2
   Act 3 scene 3
   Act 3 scene 5
   Act 5 scene 1
   Act 5 scene 3

Juliet

Juliet does not begin the play with the same thoughts and
feelings about love as Romeo and while she is just as deeply in
love with him as he with her, she thinks and speaks about it
differently. Research what love means to Juliet.

Other characters

You should also examine what these characters
understand by love:
Capulet and Lady Capulet
Paris
Nurse
Friar Lawrence
Mercutio and Benvolio

Why did Romeo and Juliet die?

Fate

The play begins with a description of Romeo and Juliet as fated to die: 'a pair of star-cross'd lovers'. There are many references to fate, the stars, and destiny:

Act 1 scene 4 lines 106-111
Act 2 scene 6 line 7
Act 3 scene 5 lines 54-56
Act 5 scene 1 lines 6, 24
Act 5 scene 3 lines 82, 111-112, 153-154

Look up all these references . For each one write down briefly: who the speaker is; the situation in which they are speaking; what they say.

Coincidence

In the plot of the play, fate works by means of coincidence. It is a coincidence that Capulet should send out the invitations to the feast using a messenger who cannot read, at just the moment when he will meet Romeo and so ask him to read the list for him (Act 1 scene 2 lines 57-83). Similarly it is a coincidence that at a crowded party, where there are many attractive young women, Romeo catches sight of Juliet (Act 1 scene 5 lines 43-52).

There are many other coincidences that lead to the deaths of the two lovers. Make a list of them and the points in the play at which they occur.

Choice

Romeo and Juliet made decisions at different points in the play. Romeo chose to go back to the Capulets' house and meet Juliet; they chose to meet again and marry. Go through the play and find the *moments of decision*. Make a list of them and the points in the play at which they occur.

Whose fault?

Another way of looking at this question is to ask who was most guilty for the deaths of Romeo and Juliet. As we have seen, they took decisions which led to their deaths, but this is only part of the story. They behaved as they did because of the situation they found themselves in and because of the way in which people treated them.

There is almost no one in the play who does not bear some responsibility for the deaths of Romeo and Juliet. Even the Prince could be accused: if he had been stronger and had tried harder to prevent the feud between the two families continuing, then the fight between Mercutio and Tybalt would not have happened. Then Romeo would not have killed Tybalt and so would not have been punished; Friar Lawrence's complicated plans would not have been necessary and the tragedy would have been avoided.

Look at the responsibility of each of these characters for the deaths of the two lovers:

Capulet
Lady Capulet
Montague
Tybalt
Mercutio
Benvolio
Nurse
Friar Lawrence.

For each one, make a list of these points:

- how they contributed to the general situation between the Montagues and the Capulets
- things they did which contributed directly to the tragedy
- things they failed to do which might have helped to avoid it.

Youth and age

> ... old folks, many feign as they were dead –
> Unwieldy, slow, heavy and pale as lead.

You may think that some parts of this play are sexist. In this speech, Juliet is clearly ageist as well! The contrasts and conflicts of young and old are an important theme in *Romeo and Juliet*. At the end of the play this is symbolised by the older members of the two families standing over the dead bodies of their two children and vowing to set up a memorial to them.

Parents and children

Think about the picture we get of family life from the play. In particular, look again at these scenes and lines:

The Montagues

Act 1 scene 1 lines 102–157; Act 5 scene 3 lines 209–211 (Some people think that the real reason why Lady Montague died was because the boy actor playing this part was also playing another part in this scene, perhaps Paris' Page.); Act 5 scene 3 lines 295–303.

The Capulets

Act 1 scene 2 lines 1–45; Act 1 scene 3; Act 3 scene 4; Act 3 scene 5 lines 64–204; Act 4 scene 2; Act 4 scene 3; Act 4 scene 4; Act 4 scene 5; Act 5 scene 3 lines 189–206, 295–303.

Consider these questions:

- What did the parents think were their responsibilities towards their children?
- How were the children expected to behave towards their parents?
- How emotionally close were the children to their parents?
- What were the different roles of the father and mother in the family?
- What are the similarities and the differences between the two families?

The extended family

The importance of the family extended far beyond the relationship between parents and children. Look at the scene between Capulet and Tybalt (Act 1 scene 5 lines 53-91). What does this tell us about the position and power of Capulet as head of a large and wealthy extended family?

The Nurse

Important scenes to look at:
Act 1 scene 3 (especially lines 16-48); Act 1 scene 5 lines 127-141; Act 2 scene 4 lines 144-214; Act 2 scene 5; Act 3 scene 2 lines 32-143; Act 3 scene 5 lines 126-242; Act 4 scene 5 lines 1-95.
Questions to think about:
● What has been the history of the Nurse's relationship with Juliet up to the beginning of the play?
● How close are she and Juliet in Act 1?
● Bearing in mind that she is employed by the Capulets, why does she behave as she does in Act 2 scenes 4 and 5 and Act 3 scene 2?
● How do you judge her behaviour in Act 3 scene 5?
● Is the Nurse a consistent character, or does she behave in an erratic way?

Friar Lawrence

Important scenes to look at:
Act 2 scenes 3 and 6; Act 3 scene 3; Act 4 scene 1; Act 5 scene 3.
Questions to think about:
● What has been the history of the Friar's relationship with Romeo up to the beginning of the play?
● Sometimes during the play he acts towards Romeo as a priest. At other times he is more like a father figure. Which of these roles is more important at each stage and why?

Character activities

One of the most important things to do when studying a play is to get to know the characters really well. Keeping Character logs as you work through the play will give you plenty of raw material, but it also important to gain a picture of each character as a whole. The activities on the next four pages will help you do this.

'Family' circles

Characters in a play can be grouped in many different ways. One way is to draw a chart showing the character's circles of affection and relationship. Write the character's name at the centre of a series of concentric circles. Then place other characters on the circles, according to how 'close' they are to that character, for example:

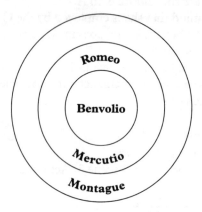

Arrows of influence

This works in a similar way, but its purpose is to show which characters had most influence (good or bad) on the central character. You show the influence by arrows: the stronger the influence the thicker the arrow (see over):

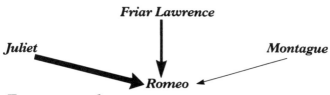

Temperature chart

This is a way of showing how events affect the character as the play proceeds. You choose a character and a quality to illustrate: for example in the case of Romeo it might be 'happiness'. You then draw a chart to illustrate how his mood changes from scene to scene:

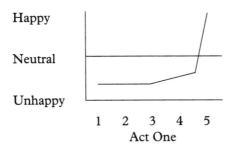

Secret files

In any play, the writer presents us with key moments in the lives of the characters and leaves us to work out the rest of their lives for ourselves. It is interesting to ask questions about those parts of the characters' lives that the writer does not tell us about. For example: what kind of home does Mercutio come from? What does the Nurse do all day?

1 Choose one of the main characters.
2 Make up a list of questions about that character that you would like answered.
3 Build up a complete 'secret file' about your chosen character. Start with their childhood and go on adding information up to the end of the play.
4 You can make up as much as you like, provided nothing contradicts the facts of the play and the behaviour of your character in it.

Quotables

When you are talking or writing about a character, it is important to be able to back up your ideas by referring to the play: 'This is true of this character, because in Act 1 scene 2 she says this, or does that.' You should have plenty of this information for the main characters in your Character logs. It is useful to keep some of this information in your head. A way of doing this is to search for 'the ideal quotation' for each character - the one line that absolutely sums up him or her . For example when the Nurse asks Romeo who Mercutio is, he replies, 'A gentleman ... that loves to hear himself talk'. Romeo thinks that sums up Mercutio - do you?

1 For each of the main characters find at least two short quotations of this kind - they may be something the character says or something another character says about them.
2 Go through your list and choose the best one for each character.
3 Work in a group and try out your quotations on the others. Make a group list of the best quotation for each character.

Comparisons

This play is full of characters who are similar yet different. It is very revealing to compare such characters and to make lists of their similarities and differences. For example, you might compare Tybalt and Mercutio:
Now make a similar comparison for one of these pairs of

Similarities	Differences
skilful	Tybalt is a Capulet, but Mercutio
swordsmen	doesn't belong to either family
young	Mercutio would rather talk than
arrogant	fight; Tybalt would rather fight than
	talk.

characters:
- Mercutio and Benvolio
- Nurse and Friar Lawrence
- Montague and Capulet
- Benvolio and Romeo
- Romeo and Juliet

Guilty parties

At the end of the play, the Prince says 'all are punished'. Presumably he means to imply that 'all are guilty of the tragic deaths of Romeo and Juliet'. But are they? If you have done the work on page 273 'Whose fault?', you will have covered some aspects of this question and will probably find the notes you made then useful now.

You can do this activity on your own, or in a group.
1 Choose a character from the list below.
2 Imagine that your chosen character is to be 'tried' for responsibility for the deaths of Romeo and Juliet.
3 Make up a prosecution case for the trial:
    - list the main reasons for their responsibility
    - for each reason list the witnesses you will call to prove your point.
4 Make up the defence case and do the same thing.
5 You could choose one or more characters for the whole class to 'try' in full.

Characters
Capulet
Montague
Friar Lawrence
Nurse
Mercutio
Tybalt
Benvolio
Prince Escalus

Writing about the play

Much of the writing you have been asked to do on the 'Activities' pages of this book has been personal or imaginative: telling the reader about your own response to an aspect of the play, or imagining that you were one of the characters in it. There is another kind of writing you will be asked to do, and that is writing about the play in a more formal way, for example:

| *Who was most responsible for the deaths of Romeo and Juliet?* |

At first this kind of writing may seem rather daunting. It can certainly be difficult to prepare for and organise. The notes on these two pages are designed to help.

The question

What you must remember – first, last and all the time – is that you have been asked a particular question. You have not been asked to 'write all you know about *Romeo and Juliet*'. So at all stages of your work you must focus on the question. And there are two key questions you should ask yourself about it:

1 Am I sure that I understand what it means?
2 What is the best way to go about answering it?

Information and ideas

Before you can plan your writing in any detail, there are two things you need to do:

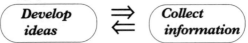

Each of these helps the other. Build up ideas by:
- talking to other people
- jotting down lists
- making a web diagram.

As you do so, you will begin to think of the information that you need. It is important to be able to back up each point you want to make by referring to something in the play - an action or a speech. You can use your Scene and Character logs to help here. As you look at the logs and at the play itself you will begin to develop new ideas.

Making a plan

Some people can write well without making a plan, but more formal writing such as this is difficult to do well without any plan at all. This is one way of planning:

1 Make a list of the main points you want to make. In the question opposite, you might decide that what you have to do is to take all the main characters in the play and examine how responsible each one was for the deaths of Romeo and Juliet.

2 Think of the best order to arrange these in. Remember that someone is going to read what you write; you need to keep their interest, so don't, for example, use up all your good ideas at the beginning so that the second half of your writing is boring. Try to make sure that one point leads naturally to the next.

3 Your last paragraph should state clearly your answer to the question - which you should have proved by everything else you have written.

4 Your first paragraph should introduce the topic - but don't give the game away at the very beginning!

The right tone of voice

If you are used to writing in personal and imaginative ways, you may find it difficult to get the right tone of voice for this kind of writing. As with other writing, it is important to think about the kind of person you are writing for. If it is an exam or test question, then you may well be writing for someone you have never met. It may help you to imagine that your reader is a teacher from another school, someone who isn't used to your way of writing and who doesn't know how you have been studying the play (and who doesn't necessarily share your sense of humour)!

Writing topics

Sometimes you may be asked to write a short response to a
question or topic, while at other times you may be required to
write at greater length. The topics on the following pages give
practice in both.

Short answers

Each of these topics requires detailed attention to a particular
scene or part of a scene. The section referred to is stated at
the beginning of each one.

1 **Act 1 scene 1**
  What are our main impressions at the end of this first
  scene, and how does Shakespeare achieve them?

2 **Act 1 scene 3**
  What do we learn in this scene about women's attitudes to
  love and marriage?

3 **Act 2 scenes 1 and 2**
  Compare the ways in which Mercutio, Romeo and Juliet
  speak of love.

4 **Act 2 scene 3**
  This is the first time we meet Friar Lawrence. What are
  our first impressions of him and how reliable are these as a
  guide to his actions later in the play?

5 **Act 3 scene 1**
  Whose fault is it that Mercutio dies?

6 **Act 3 scene 5**
  Is Capulet's outburst against Juliet expected, or
  unexpected?

7 **Act 3 scene 3 and Act 4 scene 1**
Compare the ways in which Romeo and Juliet take their problems to Friar Laurence. What does this tell us about their characters?

8 **Act 5 scene 3**
How do you judge the behaviour of Capulet and Montague at the end of the play, when they express their grief and decide to build statues of the two lovers?

Long answers

1 **Youth and age**
'Old folks ... feign as they were dead ... ' Choose any two of the older characters in the play and explain in what ways their behaviour contributed to the tragedy of Romeo and Juliet.

2 **Love**
'If love be blind ... ' Choose one character from each column, and compare and contrast their attitudes towards love:

Juliet	Mercutio
Romeo	Capulet
Benvolio	Lady Capulet
	Nurse
	Friar Laurence

3 **Fate or coincidence?**
Some people find the second half of this play difficult to take; there are just too many coincidences. Others argue that this is the whole point; Shakespeare wanted to show the workings of fate in the lives of Romeo and Juliet, and fate works through coincidence. Who do you think is right and why?

4 **Mercutio and Tybalt**

The traditional way of looking at these two characters
is to see Tybalt as a villain and Mercutio as a hero.
You could argue that Mercutio has a number of faults
(including enjoying taunting and fighting Tybalt) and
Tybalt has a number of virtues (including his fierce
loyalty to his family). What do you think is a balanced
judgement of the two men?

5 **Romeo and Juliet**

One way of measuring whether a character in a work
of literature is well-drawn is to examine how that
character changes and develops. What developments
do you see in the characters of the two lovers in the
course of *Romeo and Juliet?*

Glossary

Alarum: A call to arms, often a trumpet call.

Alliteration: A figure of speech in which a number of words close to each other begin with the same sound: *When the sun sets the earth doth drizzle dew.* Alliteration helps to draw attention to these words.

Anachronism: In a historical drama the writer may accidentally or deliberately allow characters to refer to things from a later period, which they would not have known about. This is called 'anachronism':

BRUTUS: Peace, count the clock.

CASSIUS: The clock hath stricken three.

Julius Caesar: Clocks had not been invented in Caesar's time.

Antithesis: A figure of speech in which the writer brings two opposite or contrasting ideas up against each other:

My only love sprung from my only hate!
Too early seen unknown and known too late!

Apostrophe: When a character suddenly speaks directly to someone or something, which may or may not be present:

O true Apothecary

Thy drugs are quick!

Blank verse: See page 266.

Dramatic irony: A situation in a play when the audience (and possibly some of the characters) know something that one or more of the characters don't. In a pantomime, for example, young children will often shout to tell the hero that a dreadful monster is creeping up behind him, unseen. An example from *Romeo and Juliet* is the beginning of Act 3 scene 2, when Juliet is waiting impatiently for Romeo to come to her on their wedding night. We know - and she

does not - that he has killed Tybalt and been banished
from Verona.

Exeunt: A Latin word meaning 'They go away', used for
the departure of characters from a scene.

Exit: A Latin word meaning 'He (or she) goes away',
used for the departure of a character from a scene.

Hyperbole: Deliberate exaggeration, for dramatic effect.
For example when Juliet thinks that the Nurse is
saying that Romeo is dead, she says:
What devil art thou that dost torment me thus?
This torture should be roared in dismal hell.

Irony: When someone says one thing and means
another, often to make fun of, tease, or satirise
someone else:
For Brutus is an honourable man,
So are they all, all honourable men.

Metaphor: A figure of speech in which one person, or
thing, or idea is described as if it were another. When
Capulet is furious with Juliet's refusal to marry Paris,
he tells her that he will disown her:
Graze where you will, *you shall not house with me.*
He is speaking to her as if she were no more than an
animal that eats grass and lives out in the fields. This
shows his contempt for her.

Onomatopoeia: Using words that are chosen because
they mimic the sound of what is being described:
... *'banishèd'?*
O Friar, the damnèd use that word in hell.
Howling *attends it.*
The word 'howling' makes the sound that Romeo
hears in his head when he thinks of his grief and of the
sound that lost souls make in hell.

Oxymoron: A figure of speech in which the writer
combines two ideas that are opposites. This frequently
has a startling or unusual effect:
Feather of lead, bright smoke, cold fire, sick health.

Personification: Referring to a thing or an idea as if it were a person:

Come, gentle night. Come, loving, black-browed night,
Give me my Romeo.

Play on words: see **Pun**

Pun: A figure of speech in which the writer uses a word that has more than one meaning. Both meanings of the word are used to make a joke. When Mercutio knows he is dying he says:

Ask for me tomorrow, and you shall find me a grave man.

He uses the word 'grave' to mean both 'serious' and 'dead and buried - in his grave'.

Sometimes a pun may be used to make a more serious point. When Juliet thinks that the Nurse is telling her that Romeo is dead, she asks her to confirm the news:

Say thou but 'Ay',
And that bare vowel 'I' shall poison more
Than the death-darting eye of cockatrice.
I am not I, if there be such an 'I'
Or those eyes shut that makes thee answer 'Ay'.

Simile: A comparison between two things which the writer makes clear by using words such as 'like' or 'as':

I have no joy of this contract tonight.
It is too rash, too unadvised, too sudden;
Too like the lightning, *which doth cease to be*
Ere one can say 'it lightens'.

Soliloquy: When a character is alone on stage, or separated from the other characters in some way and speaks apparently to himself or herself.